THE Warrior Mind

Ancient Wisdom from the Martial Arts for Living a More Powerful Life

Jim Pritchard

with
Sharon Lindenburger

AMACOM
American Management Association
New York • Atlanta • Brussels • Chicago • Mexico City • San Francisco
Shanghai • Tokyo • Toronto • Washington, D.C.

Special discounts on bulk quantities of AMACOM books are
available to corporations, professional associations, and other
organizations. For details, contact Special Sales Department,
AMACOM, a division of American Management Association,
1601 Broadway, New York, NY 10019.
Tel.: 212-903-8316. Fax: 212-903-8083.
Website: www.amacombooks.org

This publication is designed to provide accurate and authoritative
information in regard to the subject matter covered. It is sold with the
understanding that the publisher is not engaged in rendering legal,
accounting, or other professional service. If legal advice or other expert
assistance is required, the services of a competent professional person
should be sought.

Library of Congress Cataloging-in-Publication Data

Pritchard, Jim.
    The warrior mind : ancient wisdom from the martial arts for living a more
powerful life / Jim Pritchard with Sharon Lindenburger.
        p.   cm.
    Includes index.
    ISBN 0–8144–7303–2 (pbk.)
    1. Martial arts—Philosophy.   2. Martial arts—Psychological aspects.
    I. Lindenburger, Sharon.   II. Title.

GV1101.P75   2006
796.8'01—dc22   2005020262

Printing number

10   9   8   7   6   5   4   3   2   1

The Warrior Mind

Contents

Foreword

I have known Jim Pritchard for over twenty years. We are long-time sparring partners and have even taught in the same dojo. I can tell you from first-hand and sometimes painful experience that Jim is a formidable foe. They don't confer the rank of Shadow Warrior on just anyone, you know.

Jim's a great teacher, too. One time he graciously invited me to spar with some of his students. I declined with even greater graciousness. "Thanks but no thanks, Jim," I told him. "I really prefer to keep my eyes in my head."

You see, he always taught his charges street smarts as well as dojo smarts.

Over the years I have watched Jim help a lot of people live less fearfully and more confidently. I have watched him apply the principles and energies of his training to business and life. I am very pleased to see that he has captured all this so clearly and compellingly in this book.

Jim has developed his own way of teaching the ancient wisdom of the martial arts. He has come to believe that a person does not have to be a formal student of martial arts to apply the energies that martial artists use to deal with psychological conflicts and challenges.

Jim feels that each and every one of us wants to feel inwardly safe, to go through life with a calm center, to take a balanced approach to everything we do. His approach of "Thought + Motion = No Room for Fear" is simple yet powerful. When set in the context of the six energies he describes in this book, this approach provides the secret to mastering fear and anxiety and living a more powerful life.

In addition, Jim's work, wit, and wisdom help people gain more confidence in themselves, and an optimistic way of looking at the world—a way that balances the physical and the psychological, the mental and the spiritual.

It is my hope, and expectation, that you will find courage and inspiration within the pages of Jim's book. I know you're going to find his practical suggestions helpful in many areas of your life.

All in all, you're in good hands. (Jim has a gentle side, too.)

Wayne Erdman
Kitchener, Ontario
Gold medalist in judo at the 1975 Pan American Games
and participant in judo at the 1976 Montreal Olympics

Preface

To those of you who accept the risks of taking on challenges, this book's for you.

To those of you who have been on intimate terms with anxiety, doubt, and fear, this book's for you.

And to those of you who have known the mental clarity of creative thinking, the thrill of overcoming adversities, and the sweet taste of physical, psychological, emotional, spiritual, and financial success, this book's for you.

Acknowledgments

I want to recognize the following people for their many contributions toward completing this book:

My life partner, Grace, whose patience and life skills were demonstrated so many times during the writing of this book by her ability to stay in the here and now.

My scribe, author, and adviser, Sharon Lindenburger, who was unfamiliar with the martial arts world when we began this journey a few years ago, but can now say that she has a skilled knowledge of how we think.

My literary agent, Donald G. Bastian of Bastian Publishing Services, who has shown extraordinary skills in explaining to me the intricacies of the publishing industry.

My publisher, AMACOM, in New York City, and in particular Jacquie Flynn and her support staff, whose guidance and understanding helped ease a first-time author's trials and tribulations.

Jim Pritchard

The Warrior Mind

Introduction

I was in Newport, Rhode Island, walking alone down a poorly lit street late at night near the waterfront—a very nasty part of town. It was the kind of thing you do when you're young and tough and you think you're invulnerable.

Not surprisingly in a neighborhood like this, there are characters who have only your wallet, not your best interests, at heart. In particular, about 100 feet in front of me, two very rough-looking men were casing me from the opposite side of the street. They crossed to my side of the street. So I crossed to the other side. They crossed back and I crossed again.

In the first phases of defense taught in specialized martial arts, creative thinking takes you to the three strategies of avoid, confuse, and dissuade. When it became obvious to me that I wasn't going to avoid these individuals successfully, this mind-set prompted me to move to confuse. So I headed directly toward them and took my hands out of my pockets. I undid my jacket and put my hand inside—body language suggesting that I might have a weapon (which I didn't, except for my hands).

Their demeanor immediately changed. I had successfully confused them. They had figured that since there were two of them and only one of me, I wouldn't take them on.

Then, as I continued walking toward them, I picked out the one I thought was the leader of the two and locked my eyes onto his, sending a clear message that I was fully prepared to do battle. He wanted nothing to do with it. He turned immediately to the right and his sidekick to the left, and they took off out of there. The force of my intent was enough to dissuade them from the confrontation.

In this situation, the inner resources of my years of martial arts training had come to my aid. My mind had come into a calm focus and I was able to defuse the situation in a safe way. No one was hurt, but I had disarmed my opponents just as surely as if I'd wrenched weapons from their hands. It was all done with body language and focus of intent. This, to me, is the greatest lesson from all the great martial arts traditions—that often you can defend yourself and keep yourself safe during conflict using only the power of your mind and the ability of your body to communicate a clear message.

I learned this truth in a most graphic way as a young man training in the ways of Taijitsu and studying the path of the Shadow Warrior. Masaaki Hatsumi, the 34th Grand Master of the Togakure Ryu School of Ninjitsu in Japan, had come to the United States to do some Shadow Warrior teaching. He is five feet, one inch tall and weighs around 110 pounds. At the time, I was six feet, two inches tall and weighed 230 pounds. I was well muscled, confident, and well trained. I prided myself on the high level of martial arts skills I had already attained.

Hatsumi looked at me and began telling me that the way of the Shadow Warrior is about energy, not about strength. As I moved to spar with him, he reached out with just one finger, and suddenly I was flat on my ass on the mat. He did this to me three times.

I remember lying on the floor looking up at the ceiling and wondering what had hit me. But nothing had hit me!

That experience was a turning point for me. I learned that the most effective way to defuse conflict, and even more important, to master fear, comes from the energy inside you—that if you can tap into that energy, you can take someone bigger and more powerful than yourself down to the mat, whether physically or psychologically. I saw that the martial arts path I had been on was much wider than I thought, involving much more than sparring in dojos and gaining belts.

But it wasn't until later, after I had left the military and had spent many years honing the martial skills of the Shadow Warrior, that I began to see the implications for all of life of the wisdom emanating from these ancient martial arts. I began teaching people how to use these energies to help them handle their challenges from a calm center within themselves. And not just handle them in the sense of merely coping, but actually to move from surviving to thriving. They were able not only to get through difficulties but also to actively engage all their inner resources to conquer whatever it was that was frightening them the most.

I found that a constellation of principles had arranged themselves in my consciousness into a pattern of six "moves" that individually, in various combinations, or in their totality when the situation really requires it, can address just about any challenge in life. Even though I speak of them as moves, and sometimes their expression does involve movement, they are more accurately called *energies*. These energies are drawn upon and used by your mind. The names of these energies are not officially from Taijitsu, or other martial practices, but emerged from within me, names that captured my own expe-

rience of them and translated them to a wider context. Here
they are:

1. **Attentive Curiosity:** the ability to observe calmly what
    is going on in your situation, including the unseen or
    less obvious aspects.

2. **Undulation:** a side-to-side flowing energy, which as
    a physical movement is an extremely effective self-
    defense move, and as a mental energy helps to free up
    your inner creativity and resourcefulness.

3. **Clear Intent:** knowing exactly what you want.

4. **Grappling:** the ability to "take on" a situation and ac-
    tively engage with whatever is going on in your life.

5. **Rolling Waves:** a targeted persistence that follows the
    rhythm of taking action, withdrawing to see what hap-
    pens, then taking another action—similar to how ocean
    waves flow in and out.

6. **The Whirlwind:** pulling out all the stops; a complete
    onslaught to solving a problem or resolving a situation;
    the "take no prisoners" energy.

The very good news is that these six energies can empower
you to face and overcome your life's challenges. By a shift in
your body's energies and a corresponding shift in your mind,
you can learn to feel safer in your own skin and deal confidently with anything life throws your way. The energies will
help you convert an anxious, troubling, or challenging situa-

tion into one you feel safe to handle. They will help you stay focused and grounded. They will help you defend yourself in conflict (physical, psychological, or spiritual), operate effectively under stress, and get in touch with strengths within that you may not have realized you have.

Before we look at where we will be journeying together in this book, allow me a few words about my background.

From a very early age, self-defense training (both physical and psychological) has been a big part of my life. I was born in northern Canada and began my self-defense disciplines at the age of 10 under the tutelage of a former member of the French Foreign Legion, who was boarding in my family's home. After high school, I decided I wanted to join the military. I joined the Canadian navy in the early 1960s. After training as a clearance diver, I volunteered to train with U.S. armed forces in shooting, jumping, explosives, underwater operations, and reconnaissance. As a member of U.S. Special Forces, I did tours of duty and exchanges in Southeast Asia, Australia, the United Kingdom, and South America. After my active service, I continued to perform many training assignments in various parts of the world and furthered my lifelong practice in martial arts.

While in Special Forces I learned much about the reality of conflict—how to do battle, how to calm the effects of conflict, and how to acquire and understand the delicate psychological balance between conflict and safety. I became a peacemaker. What I have learned has been tempered by my lifelong interest in Eastern philosophies and the pursuit of martial arts disciplines, and how to mix the wisdom of the East with the orientation of the West.

Dr. Masaaki Hatsumi was a major influence in my life. Not only did he teach me the power of energy, but he also guided me to understand what inner strength really is. I adopted the Ninjitsu skills of the Togakure Ryu tradition to complement my existing skills in Taijitsu and Jujitsu. Today I continue to practice the ways of the Shadow Warrior, which involve highly advanced levels of consciousness training, meditation, and awareness.

After my honorable discharge from the military in the late 1970s, I turned to the business field, working in management training, sales, and sales management with several international companies. In the mid-1980s, I became an entrepreneur and established an industrial distributorship. My company, Kit-Fast Solutions Inc., which I have now sold in order to concentrate my energies on writing and teaching, expanded its market and range of products to service a large number of clients in the United States, Canada, the Caribbean, and South America. It wasn't long before I discovered that business has many situations where the six energy moves come in mighty handy.

My preferred martial practice involves using the skills of the Shadow Warrior to understand the influences of both passive and overt actions. Living as a Shadow Warrior is about knowing how to stay safe both inwardly and outwardly when faced with a challenge, how to defuse conflict, and how to understand and use personal power. My life's path has led me to become a specialist in understanding and deterring psychological violence and to turn those learnings into a deeper wisdom.

But you don't have to be a Shadow Warrior to access the six energies I'm talking about. You can learn them in your own life. They do not require lengthy training. They do not require athletic skill (although they do require practice). They are energies you feel in your body, but they are not solely physical in their expression. This is a most important point because 99 percent of the time you will use your mind to apply one or more of the energy moves to the mental, emotional, or spiritual issues in your life.

I have taught these six energies to groups and individuals in business settings, community settings, empowerment workshops, and self-defense and safety training; and in helping people to deal with difficult issues in their personal lives, including recovering from sexual assault. The moves can change your life by connecting you to what inner safety and focused balance really feel like and by helping you make these manifest in your life.

Here's where we're headed together in this book:

- Chapter 1 looks at the desire we all have for inner safety.

- Chapter 2 explains the six energies in greater detail and gives you a picture of how they can work in your life.

- Chapter 3 discusses how you can train your mind to use the six energies consciously to change the way you think about things. It all begins in the mind.

- Chapter 4 shows how the energies can help you in the everyday routine challenges that can be anything but routine in the amount of anxiety they engender.

- Chapter 5 demonstrates how these six energies can help you in your job or business.

- Chapter 6 describes how the six energies can help you in your relationships.

- Chapter 7 shows you how to carry yourself like a Shadow Warrior. We'll look at how to use the six energies in physical self-defense situations to protect your body so that you can increase your sense of physical safety and know what to do if you feel you are in physical danger.

- Chapter 8 concludes the book by looking at the relationship of these six energies to all of your life. It discusses what gives meaning to your life and shows you how to deal with the big questions.

I like a phrase used in a TV commercial for Adidas with footage of the great boxer Muhammad Ali and his daughter, a champion boxer herself. The three-word slogan captures what I think is the very essence of a courageous and empowered life: "Impossible is Nothing." If you allow yourself to play with the energies of the six moves I'm going to be talking about, you'll find that impossible really *is* nothing. And that life is a vast field of possibilities and opportunities where you can and will handle anything that comes your way.

CHAPTER 1

Looking for Inner Safety

I'll never forget one of the scariest experiences I had in the military. I was sixty feet below the surface of the Caribbean Sea, just off the coast of Antigua. I was with a dive team participating in a NATO exercise when we were given orders to do a grid search for a downed military aircraft that had crashed into the sea. We had been searching for about an hour when my air supply began running low. I turned on my reserve air and began to follow my air bubbles up.

But then I heard a most unwelcome sound: a whoosh of air escaping. The incoming air hose had detached from its cradle in my mouthpiece. Instead of air I got a mouthful of saltwater. "Uh-oh!" I thought, "this is not good." I did have a very serious problem. I was down far too deep, and carrying too much weight in equipment, to hold my breath for the time I would need to get to the surface.

In that moment of fear, the inner resources of my years of military and martial arts training kicked in. My mind came into a calm focus. My right arm brought the undulating air hose under control as I grabbed the end that had broken away. I was able to guide air from the hose so that it was flowing over my lips. By breathing in gently, my lungs filled with air instead of seawater. And then, with no time to spare, I rose to the surface. I made it, but only just.

In the Grip of Fear

Though it may not be as dramatic as being stuck under the sea with a faulty air hose, all of us experience times when we find ourselves in the cold, hard grip of fear. It can happen to us in our work lives, our home lives, our emotional lives, or our spiritual lives. Sometimes we can see clearly what the challenge is—competition at work, a failing relationship, a serious health problem, a business setback, a conflict with another person. Other times we can't quite name it. We just carry, everywhere we go, a life-sapping burden of anxiety. Nothing seems right.

Whether the perceived threats are external or internal, it all comes down to having a constant, nagging feeling of being "unsafe," a feeling that we have lost our bearings, that we are buffeted by other people's agendas or blindsided by the curveballs life is throwing at us.

The feeling of inner safety can be elusive. Many parts of our world are war torn and violent, and the prospect of peace seems very far away. Crime rates rise in our cities and we worry about the possibility of being assaulted, mugged, stalked, robbed, maybe even murdered. Despite the fact that companies draft and attempt to implement antiharassment policies, we feel under siege in our jobs, either from the stress of the job itself or from all the conflicts and intrigue that go on in most workplaces today. Schools design programs to combat bullying, but just ask students whether they feel safe there. We are frightened of terrorism, terrified of possible epidemics, worried about job loss. We encounter road rage; rude sales-clerks; and cold, impersonal bankers.

Competitiveness is the rule in so many areas of life that there seems to be no place where you can just be you. Even your intimate relationships are marked by power struggles and suffer from the psychological residue of your daily strug-gles "out in the world." Yet you accept all this stress as just being the way things are. Of course there are external things you can do, such as install an alarm system in your house or car, carry pepper spray in your purse, or triple lock your door at night. But feeling safe involves much more than depen-dency on external gadgets. What you need to know is that the safety you long for is not external to you. It is inside you.

What Fear Is

One thing that can totally permeate your mind and color all your experiences is the feeling or perception of fear. I cannot tell you what fear is for *you*. The experience of fear is different for everyone. But I can tell you what fear is in general and what it *does* to all of us.

Fear is a response to a circumstance in your life that trig-gers defenses that in turn tell you you're weak in a certain area. You're vulnerable. You're insecure. The situation doesn't feel safe.

Fear occurs when you're in a situation where you feel over-whelmed, or outnumbered, or threatened, or intimidated, or not up to a challenge, or anxious because of something new or unexpected in your environment. You have the feeling of "I'm not up to dealing with this," and your mind is screaming at you to get out of there. You're in the fight/flight syndrome. You want to leave and get into an environment where you don't feel quite so vulnerable. Then comes that moment when you realize you can't leave. You're there. So what are you going to do about it?

Have you ever noticed that when you're experiencing fear your breathing seizes up? It gets shallow. Sometimes you even hold your breath. Or you hyperventilate. Fear locks you up. You feel like you can't move—you're frozen. But what you need to know is that you can change where your thoughts are focused. You can move them from the chill of fear to a state of having them just be there before you as something you look at within your attentive curiosity, knowing that you do have choices. You're not stuck without any choice whatsoever. You even have the choice of remaining fearful. When you're feeling fear, your traditional defenses don't work. They won't come to your aid. So when your inner defenses are incapable of helping you, this should be telling you that you should be looking for something else, for another way.

Fear and anxiety often just seem to strike out of the blue. Let's say you've prepared a great marketing proposal and you're about to present it to your manager or to your company's CEO. All of a sudden, you have a lump in your throat and butterflies in your gut. That's your "friend" fear. That's the time when your mind decides that you should be paralyzed by anxiety and become a bumbling idiot when normally you are a well-spoken individual. Your fear shuts off the brain's messages to your tongue and you stand there sputtering. You become ensconced in the fear because you don't understand why it happened. You think, "I'm in a spiral and it's only going in one direction—downhill!"

You can't get rid of fear. It's part of the human condition. It's your natural response to a perception of threat or vulnerability. And let's face it, when you're in front of the brass making that presentation, you *are* vulnerable—you're putting yourself on the line.

It can be something as simple as crossing at a stoplight. You see the traffic going by, and as soon as the light turns green for you, you see some guy in his car barreling across the intersection through the red light. Your body goes into the flight response and you immediately jump back. Your heart pounds. In this case, fear is the system warning you that you are in an unsafe situation. But the problem is that you may carry the anxiety about this "near miss" around with you all day, and you might even find yourself a few days later being nervous about crossing at a stoplight on a deserted street. That fear, that nervousness, is interfering with your ability to feel safe inside yourself.

There are so many situations in life in which we are afraid because of something that happened in the past that we may not even remember. That's how the mind can trick us into a fear state instead of returning us to a state of inner stability.

The bad news is you can't totally eliminate fear. The good news is you *can* learn to function *despite* the fear. The mind must be trained to get us into that peaceful state and to keep us in that state.

What Is Safety?

Many people think safety is lack of risk, but that's not accurate. All of life is risk. The minute you get out of bed in the morning, you face so many risks. You could fall and sprain your ankle running for a bus. You could come down with a cold that's been spreading around your workplace. You could make a disaster out of a new recipe.

Safety is the inner knowledge that if you come up against a risky circumstance, you have the good clear thinking that enables you to either back away from that circumstance or deal with it. Being safe is knowing that when you're called into your manager's office to do that presentation you can do it, knowing that everything you are contributing is your best effort and that there is no such thing as perfection. Safety is knowing that no matter what you do, you can be comfortable with it because you have the smarts to accept the challenge and you also have the smarts to reject a challenge when necessary, and that you know when to do which.

Now here's where your mind gets into the act. The minute your mind perceives that a "risk" is putting you in harm's way, it starts screaming at you, "What are you doing? You're taking a risk! It's just too much! Don't do that!" If the risk in question really is a potentially threatening situation—for example, if your mind tells you that it's not a good idea to walk through a tough neighborhood in your city alone late at night—then the caution of your mind is serving you well.

But how many times does our mind tell us not to do something, and when we really look at it, it's not so threatening after all and in fact may be just the thing we need to do? Learning to overcome an unreasonable fear and to get to a place of inner safety is to do it anyway. We need to draw closer to the concept of experience, to what the energy in the situation feels like. Once we connect with the experience, the risk we feel and the fear we feel become an energy. Jumping out of an airplane will be an experience. Doing a presentation at work will be an experience.

The Difference Between Risk and Danger

Often taking a risk feels like being in danger. What really is danger? You have jumped out of a plane at 10,000 feet, you're now passing through 7,000 feet—heading into 5,000, then 4,000, then 3,000 feet—and it's time to pop your chute. You go to put your fingers in the D-ring and you can't find it. That's danger! Danger is a situation of imminent disaster. The *Oxford Dictionary* defines it as "liability or exposure to harm or death." Danger is when you know that the likelihood of something very bad happening is very high. When I was sixty feet under the ocean with a broken air hose, as I described earlier, *that's danger.*

But many of us perceive "danger" when we are simply in uncomfortable situations. The lack of comfort translates in our mind to "danger," and our fear detector goes way up. Public speaking is a great example of this. Some surveys have shown that people fear it more than they fear death. I know a person who every time he gets up to speak in public breaks out into a cold, clammy sweat. He is certain that everyone can see the wet patches under his armpits. He feels like he's in front of a firing squad.

Risk and danger may be related in the sense that some risks can lead to danger, but they are not the same thing. You know that every time you get into a car, there's a risk that you could have an accident. But if you're in the car and another driver is coming straight at you in a skid, that's danger. There is a continuum on which risk changes into danger, and we all have different places in our mind where we make the jump from the perception of risk to the perception of danger. Some people feel endangered by minor things, and other people are so risk oriented they wouldn't perceive danger until a bayonet is running them through.

One dictionary definition of risk is "the possibility of meeting danger or suffering harm or loss." Note the word "possibility." The possibility exists that almost every circumstance can expose us to risk of some sort, and that's what gives our mind a field day to really spook us.

Let's say you have borrowed $100,000 from a bank. The bank wants everything you own as collateral to offset the risk for the bank. The truth is the bank has no risk. *You* have all the risk. If you fall behind on the payments, the bank may call the loan. So you go into that situation knowing that you have to organize and manage the risk. If you spend all your energy in an anxious state of mind, you won't be able to devote your energies to making sure that you manage the loan effectively. If you manage the loan effectively and it accomplishes what you need for your business or home renovations or whatever reason you took the loan, then your feeling of inner safety will grow stronger.

Feeling safe is a state of mind. How close do you want to get to that rattlesnake? That's risk. Being one foot from that rattlesnake and it's rattling at you and preparing to strike, that's danger. Safety is knowing that you aren't getting close to that rattlesnake. And safety is also realizing that the rattlesnake is in fact a garter snake, and not going into the fear reaction reserved for encounters with real rattlesnakes. Don't let your mind show you "rattlesnakes" in your life situation when those "snakes" are really the harmless garden variety.

Maybe they bother you, maybe you don't like them, but they can't harm you.

Reminders to Your Warrior Mind

1. Fear is a response to a circumstance in your life that triggers defenses that tell you that you are weak in a certain area. It occurs when you're in a situation where you feel overwhelmed, outnumbered, threatened, intimidated, not up to a challenge, or anxious because of something new or unexpected in your environment. You cannot get rid of fear. It is part of the human condition. But you can learn to master fear through awareness of the energies in your mind and body.

2. Safety is not lack of risk. Safety is the awareness that when you come up against a risky circumstance, there are ways you can either back away from the risk or learn to deal with it. You need to draw closer to the concept of experience, to what the energy in a situation feels like.

3. There is a difference between risk and danger. Risk is the possibility that something will be either uncomfortable or unsafe, with emphasis on "possibility." It's not a definite, merely a possibility. Danger, on the other hand, is a clear and present threat to your safety.

4. There is a continuum on which risk changes into danger, and all of us have different places in our minds where we make the jump from the perception of risk to the perception of danger. Some individuals can feel "endangered" by

very minor situations, whereas others are so risk oriented that they don't perceive danger until they are in a life-and-death situation.

5. When you are in a situation in your life that is making you anxious or uncomfortable, take a look at whether you are feeling that situation as a risk or as a danger. If you conclude that it is a risk, you may decide to take that risk or not, as the case may be. However, avoid calling a risk a "danger." Ask yourself: Am I really in serious danger here?

6. Feeling safe is a state of mind. Remember the example of the rattlesnake.

CHAPTER 2

Learning the Six Energies

Whenever I teach the six energies to people, I find that they have a great deal of anxiety, fear, and doubt in their lives and are looking for a safe place within themselves. They are looking for a way to protect themselves during conflict. What they come to realize is that through the six energies, they can learn to connect in a dynamic and very real way with their fears and doubts. And it's not just a matter of dealing with things—you know the expression, "You have to *deal* with it." No, it's actually shifting your energy to decrease the impact of fear and doubt, to lessen the sense of danger, and to sharpen your awareness so that you can protect yourself in the tight corners.

The idea is that you come to a working agreement with the six energies and come to an understanding of how and when they are relevant in your life. Once you have that understanding, then you can accept your own life—where you are, why you're there—and be comfortable with that. When you experience this comfort zone of inner safety, it is without ego. It is without vanity. As you age and progress through your life, you can invoke any of the six energies at any time to assist you—from relationships to dealing with your bank manager to your job performance to defending yourself from intimidation to dealing with life's aggravations, large or small.

I like to locate the six energies as elements on the classic Yin Yang symbol.

On the black side—the Yin side—is passive power. It's the receptive, curious side. It is there we place the energy of *attentive curiosity* and the energy of *clear intent*. *Undulation* is also there, although it can move toward the Yang side as it begins as a yielding energy and may lead us to physical action. On the white side of the circle—the Yang side, representing active power—we place *grappling, rolling waves,* and *the whirlwind.*

These energies—whether in a physical self-defense situation or a psychological situation—move very quickly. In any situation you only stay in any one of them for as long as necessary. The key is the fluidity—the ability to *move.* The formula is:

Thought + Motion = No Room for Fear

Let's walk through a situation to illustrate the six energies in action. Later on in this chapter and throughout this book, we'll be going into each of them in more detail as they are required in different situations, but for now I just want you to get an idea of how these energies move through you to get you to a place of inner safety.

Let's say that you're in sales and you have to call on a potential new client and make a sales presentation. Let's say that making presentations always makes you nervous. Your palms sweat; your breathing gets shallower; your heart beats faster. If you don't handle your anxiety, you may end up blowing your sales call.

Go into the energy or mind state that I call *attentive curiosity*. You're simply going to allow yourself to be curious about what is there before you. You're going to say to yourself, "Well, this is a new situation. Each call is a new challenge. I wonder what this one could be like." You're going to look at what is really there. You're going to watch closely and calmly, without reacting. That's what attentive curiosity is, getting "the lay of the land." When you go to that state—when attentive curiosity plays in your psyche and you allow yourself to rest in its energy—fear cannot exist. Doubt cannot exist because at that point there is nothing to doubt. Nothing has happened yet. You are receiving the impact of your environment through the attentive curiosity state of mind.

What you are doing is creating an energy that connects with your own natural curiosity. But it's not the curiosity of a child. It's the curiosity of an adult. It's attentive; it's focused on the specific circumstance. When you allow yourself to relax and focus with attentive curiosity, the energy will naturally progress to the second move—*undulation*—which is a flowing, side-to-side moving energy. As you consider this sales presentation you have to make, you notice that your attentive curiosity has taken you into a mind state that says, "Maybe this, maybe that, maybe I should try this approach, maybe I should greet the person this way, maybe we should have coffee, maybe I should be really formal, maybe, maybe, maybe. . . ."

This is mental *undulation*. It's not dithering. It's actually the natural action of your mind to help you arrive at a focus. It's not quite the same as weighing alternatives, although it may seem similar. With undulation, at this point, you're more concerned about the movement of your mind than you are about whether any of the possibilities you are thinking of make sense.

Undulation counteracts the fight/flight syndrome—the panicky feelings—because you're allowing your mind, through mental undulation, to play with possibilities. You're loosening up your energy resources. Undulation is not random; it is deliberate. As you do this, you find that you begin quite naturally to get more focused and discard thoughts that are not relevant.

Then your energy moves to the third energy step—*clear intent*. You think about the reason for your situation, which is to make that sales call. The fact that you're nervous about the sales call doesn't have anything to do with your intent. You've focused your attentive curiosity on your nervousness. You have mentally undulated through the anxious part. You have created a relationship with your anxiety that does not freeze you into immobility. You then feel an energy that says to you, "You're actually going there—to that sales presentation, to connect with that person." As you feel this sense of validating your own intent, this is your clear intent, the jumping-off point of making a decision. You feel calmer, more in control, and less anxious.

Once you're there, you're going to begin *grappling*. You grapple with the event presenting itself. You grapple with what's beyond the initial, "Hello, how are you? I'm so-and-so from company x. Nice to meet you." You know that you want this person to order your product or buy your services. You also know that you want this person to like and respect you. You look for the clues in the person's responses that will allow you to grapple with each signal he or she gives you. You grapple with the energy coming from the other person. You allow yourself to be engaged in the energy dance. Throughout the grappling phase, you keep falling back to your clear intent. Your intention is to be there and to establish a connection with your potential client.

Perhaps the person doesn't seem terribly receptive to you. Then you may find yourself back at attentive curiosity— "What can I do here?" Instead of trying to guide the conversation, you engage with what is coming at you. You grapple again by inviting the other person into the conversation.

"Yes, things are tight right now," you say. "Yes, there are a lot of other products out there. I realize it's hard to make a decision to do business with me if you've never done business with me before."

You're still grappling, only rather than struggling you're moving with the energy. You are combining your energy with that person's and blending it—which is a cornerstone of all good martial arts self-defense techniques, using your opponent's own energies to help you get the result you want.

After a period of time of doing this "energy dance" you might then say, "Is there anything I can do to help you?" or the even more powerful questions, "What would you have to be sure of in order to do business with me? What would you need to know to make you totally comfortable ordering this product from me?"

You have made a shift. You've done your grappling and now you've thrown this new comment at your client, but it's not a confrontation. It's a *rolling wave.* You let that wave flow in and then let it recede while you watch what happens. This is the energy of touching the other person with the waves of your intent—rolling in, rolling out. You have aroused the person's curiosity. You have overcome some of the person's defenses in a totally nonthreatening way. As the person answers your questions, he or she will give you the clues you need to be able to answer his or her need with your product or service. At that stage, each point you make will be a rolling wave, . . . roll in, roll out, roll in, roll out . . . just like ocean waves.

Much to your surprise you're going to come to a resolution. When you make the sale, you'll be ecstatic. But even if you don't, you will still feel good about the process. You will have felt safe within yourself all through it, rather than continually nervous and out of focus. And the chances are that if you used these energy steps well, you did make the sale.

There's a sixth energy, *the whirlwind,* which we did not use in this example. Of all the energies, the whirlwind is the one you will use least. I call it the element of last resort. It is the power of an explosive but very focused confrontation. Shock and awe, you might say. Obviously, this would not be the wisest element to draw upon during a sales call, but there are areas in your life where you may need to use the whirlwind, and we'll be talking about those areas later in the book.

But for now, in the rest of this chapter, let's look more closely at each of these six energy moves.

Attentive Curiosity

Attentive curiosity is a threshold energy. It's an energy that is open to taking in what is going on around you. In the military we call it force reconnaissance or force recon, which means you carefully and calmly observe everything around you without drawing attention to yourself. You're gathering information about the forces that are opposing you and the direction you want to go. There is much to be said for being a good observer. And the key is neither to react emotionally to what you are observing nor to ascribe any value judgments to what you see at this point. Just look calmly. Just be curious. Note the details.

Say you're out after dark in a strange city, and you encounter some strangers on a deserted street. Or you're in an elevator with strangers and the elevator stops between floors. Your first instinct is fight/flight—"Get me out of here!" But it may be the case that you have nothing to fear. Pay attention. Observe. Ask yourself, "What is it I'm afraid of?" You focus on the circumstance that is giving you the anxiety and you think, "I want to take a look at this. I'm going to be curious about this." You're an observer of your own state of mind, without reacting.

In Buddhist meditation, this is called "mindfulness," just looking at what is there, letting it be there, being curious about it. You cultivate your curiosity. This calm state of mind, which observes all, can very quickly, in some cases almost instantly, give you the clues as to whether you're actually under threat. When you can isolate yourself emotionally from the circumstance, even for a few seconds, you will find that the energies within you are ready to respond in ways that will alleviate your anxiety and allow you to take a clear and appropriate action.

Undulation

Undulation is the ability to move from side to side, and from top to bottom. Physically it's a loose, relaxed, swaying motion. Think of how a snake moves. Or a wheat field in the wind. Undulation is one of the most effective physical self-defense techniques. It doesn't depend on body strength and it will help you release yourself from anyone who has you in a strong grip. If an assailant traps your body, the undulation move allows you to use your entire body to break the hold, even if your opponent is much stronger than you are. If someone is squeezing you and you can't breathe, you'd better be able to free your mind and use your entire body weight as a weapon.

Used as a mental or psychological strategy, undulation is the process of moving in a relaxed, flowing way from one thought to another. It keeps you from getting stuck in a particular perception. It's change, change, change. It helps you escape from the sense of entrapment and it gives you a strong physical and emotional sense that there are alternative actions open to you.

A friend of mine, a business owner, got a call from the bank informing him that it was going to call in his loan. He and I talked about it. We went over everything that would be involved in this event—his role, his family's role, the bank's role, and his lawyer's role. "What happens if I do this? Can I try this? Can I try that? We have the customer orders. We just have a short-term cash flow problem. What should I tell my employees? How should I talk with the bank? Who can give me the best advice?"

I wanted our discussion to trigger his mind into this energy of undulation. Fear and anxiety lock you up. Undulation creates thought in motion. It shifts your energy. Then you can back away from your emotional reaction to the situation and experience more fluidity.

So if the bank says that it's going to call your loan, and you react by thinking, "I'll lose my house, I'll lose my business, I'll lose my reputation," stop right there. Realize that when you first get the news, none of this is happening in that moment. Realize that you've got time to work things out. You don't have to be rushed or pressured or bullied.

So with our example of the bank loan, you'll realize that the bank has to inform you of its intent with a registered letter, that you then have several days before you have to respond. Now you can put things in place to defend yourself and not be panicked. You have time to allow your mind to sway back and forth between possibilities. As you shake your fear loose by using the energy of undulation, you'll exercise your resourcefulness and creativity.

Clear Intent

After you have gone through undulation in your psychological self-defense, you have considered a number of possibilities. You have thought of ten or twelve things you could do. Now it's time for you to take it down to two or three. You say to yourself, "There are two or three things I can do that will be most effective in helping me get what I want." So now you're not focusing on the other eight or nine things. Your energy is moving you toward validating your intent to focus on the two or three or one. In other words, you have arrived at your clear intent.

In any kind of self-defense or self-protection, you have to know what your intent is. You have to come to a point of clarity of knowing exactly what it is you're going to do. If you're in physical danger, your intent is to get the hell out of there! If you're in a quandary at work or in your business, you need to know how you intend to deal with things. Don't just act blindly.

I once owned a commercial building with some partners. The occupancy was down and the property was worth less than the value of the mortgage. We had to decide what to do because all the partners were putting in money every month and the light at the end of the tunnel was a freight train!

I asked my partners, "Who of you wants to retain this circumstance in your life?" Of course, none of us did. We began to consider all the possibilities. We figured that we would have to negotiate with our bank. I said, "We have to set it up so that the bank shares the problem with us." We discussed which of us would talk to the bank, and the task fell on me. I then had a stop payment put on the mortgage check and directed my partners to refer all calls from the bank to me.

The bank manager called me and said, as any good banker would, "We can seize the property."

"Why are you telling me what I already know?" I replied. "We don't want the building anymore. You hold the mortgage. We all took a risk and we want you to be accountable for your portion of the risk. Put the property up for sale and if there is any shortfall, you come to us and we'll make up the difference."

"But, but, but . . ." the bank manager sputtered. I headed him off by saying, "Until you come up with something we can live with, this is the path we're taking."

We finally got a call to have a meeting. At the meeting I asked the bank manager, "What would you like to talk about?" We gave them the layout in terms of the arrears, the interest, and penalties, and they said, "Okay, we can do that."

What we were doing was calling the bank's bluff. While it was true that the bank could still have seized the property, we finessed the bank into taking some responsibility in partnership with us for selling the building. Either way, the bank would have been stuck with the building. This way we were able to get the resolution we needed without being strong-armed by the bank.

We looked at the situation using attentive curiosity, becoming detached from the anxiety associated with fear and loss. We undulated through all the possible scenarios. We then came to the clear intent of what we intended to do and set our plan into motion. The energy of these three steps guided us away from anxiety into a satisfactory resolution. We were all able to sleep at night. Well, maybe not the bank manager, but certainly my partners and I.

Grappling

We can all picture what grappling is. In Judo and in my preferred martial practice, Taijitsu, there are extensive grappling techniques. Some of these are very simple to learn. However, I am more interested in psychological grappling. In your life it's good to cultivate the skills of grappling because it not only is effective when done well but it can also be a lot of fun if you really let yourself get into the flow of its energy. If you know how to grapple and your opposition does not, you can *really* have some fun.

There is both a playfulness and a seriousness to grappling. It teaches you to use both the energies of your body and the energies of your mind as a weapon to defeat whatever it is that's trying to bring you down.

In Western society, there's the saying "Stand up and fight!" Wrong. One of the better places to fight from is down on the mat. It's *good* to be down on the mat. Fight from the ground up. Some of the best physical fighters I've ever seen get down on the ground, faking weakness, because now they can *really* fight. It's short; it's sweet; it's winnable.

If you know how to grapple, you have an edge over your opponent, whether physically or psychologically. People who exhibit the characteristic of bullying are doing just that—bullying—and it's not effective as a winning strategy. They don't know how to grapple. If you do know how to grapple you can keep yourself safe in the face of any kind of psychological intimidation. In grappling you come to the energy of dealing with a circumstance that requires your direct input. You identify the problem and you position yourself beneath the problem (psychologically down on the mat), and you grapple. We'll be talking much more about how to do this later in the book.

You get to be a good grappler by practicing. You can practice this in everything you do in your daily life—in how you drive your car, deliver your presentations at work, make your bank deposits, communicate with your children. When you grapple, you "take on" the issue. Good grappling helps you stack things in your favor.

In grappling you are defensive with an aggressive opponent, and you are aggressive with an elusive opponent. In driving, for example, if you've got some goof cutting you off, you don't try to outrun him. Instead, you drive *defensively,* controlling your own car and your own annoyance, so that you're driving "beneath the radar" of the other driver's aggressive driving.

In this case, your grappling takes the form of staying out of his or her way. Grappling doesn't always mean action. Sometimes you are actually grappling by doing nothing or by refusing the confrontation. Grappling is knowing when and when not to act.

Good grappling can only happen after you've been through the energy steps of attentive curiosity, undulation, and clear intent. *Then* you grapple.

We all know people who get in there and just start flailing away at the problem, attacking the wrong issue, mistaking minor details for the main problem, and so forth. That's not grappling. That's flapping. Most people are bad grapplers in their lives. So if *you* can learn to do it well, you'll have the advantage and you'll feel much safer about your world and within yourself.

Rolling Waves

Rolling waves is a technique of targeted persistence. You go forward, you pull back, you go forward, and you pull back again—just like ocean waves that never vary from this continuous motion.

Let's go back to the scenario of the bank manager calling in a loan. After considering all avenues for action, perhaps you tell the bank that your lawyer would like to understand more about its position. That's a wave. The bank manager is thrown off center and thinks, "Hey, this person plans to defend himself." The next day you come to the bank with the record of the total amount of deposits you have made into your business account over the past years, illustrating how much business the bank has done with you. That's another wave.

Then the bank manager says, "Well, we still want you to pay off the loan immediately."

So you say, "Well, if you want me to pay it off, I want a discount for the immediateness of my paying it off."

Now you've hit the bank with another wave. Rolling waves comes about from the energy going back and forth between your intent and your action, and if you learn to be open to it, you will actually feel this wavelike energy as it moves in your body and your mind. If you learn to do it calmly and relentlessly, you can prevail, or at the very least make the situation a lot easier for yourself.

In physical defense situations, rolling waves can happen very quickly. Someone has grabbed you and through undulation you've managed to break the grip. This is where it comes together in nanoseconds—maybe you throw an elbow into your opponent's solar plexus and immediately follow it with a back fist to the nose. You just keep crashing into her, like one of those waves that is 360 feet high and curls at the top. In situations like that, however, you need to judge very quickly whether rolling waves is your best strategy or whether to stick with clear intent, in which you have validated your intent to just get out of there. Don't go inviting trouble!

In psychological situations, though, the rolling waves strategy really helps you feel your own strength. Persistence is the fuel of rolling waves. You can learn to do it calmly and in a targeted fashion. Another key is not to keep throwing waves when you've accomplished your goal. Know when to stop. If your rolling waves have been effective, everyone will get the message.

The Whirlwind

The whirlwind is the most aggressive of the six energy moves. It's what I call the element of last resort. In a physical context, it's basically the action of whirling around your opponent and striking. You're searching for his weak spots and you thoroughly do what the opponent doesn't expect. There is no stopping the whirlwind.

To use a military analogy, the whirlwind is a "force multiplier." This means that instead of using just one force, such as artillery alone, we hit the enemy with artillery, airpower, naval power, ground forces, with all available force. It's like the shock-and-awe techniques used in the 2003 Iraq war. The whirlwind is designed to totally overwhelm the opponent and defend your intent.

I hope that physically or psychologically in your lifetime you don't have to get into the whirlwind, but if you do, it's available to you. It can, for example, be used in business practice, such as an all-out marketing campaign that pulls out all the stops against your competition. Or if you have a serious health condition, you may decide to take an approach that attacks the disease on all fronts. Or you may need to confront somebody openly with a lot of verbal force. In self-defense where you are physically threatened (for example, you are being followed on a dark street), you often can repel your opponent by whirling around and shouting "No!" into your assailant's face. This is often taught to women who are being harassed or followed where they are instructed to shout "fire!" as an alarm call and then get out of there.

The whirlwind is explosive, but it is not a loss of control. It's not losing your cool. It's exploding into targeted action. You are in control but your energies are that of the whirlwind, totally focused and totally in motion. As opposed to rolling waves, which roll in and recede and roll in again, the whirlwind is all around your opposition. It's total. You use it when the equilibrium in a situation can only be restored by a total onslaught.

How the Six Energies Will Help You

As you learn to feel the six energies in your body, in your mind, and in your being, you'll discover that your thinking on a lot of issues becomes more creative. You'll have more vitality, more energy available to you for your life. You'll feel safer, calmer, more focused, and more powerful. You'll know that you can handle just about any situation. These six energies take you into the realm of your own personal responsibility. They are the tools that can release you from fear and inject into your life the positive effects of focused action, no matter what your station in life is.

Each of us has a different experience of what inner safety feels like. Some people seem to be born risk takers and appear to thrive in dangerous situations. Other people are highly risk averse and seek to avoid taking chances. Most of us fall somewhere in the middle. But all of us, even the seemingly most daring risk takers, have the experience of times where we feel inwardly anxious and unsafe. When we talk about inner safety, it's not about removing all risk from your life. Risk is involved in just living. If you don't ever risk anything, you'll never accomplish your dreams or goals.

A powerful person is a centered person who knows how to use attentive curiosity in the "environment" of her life and can detect both dangers and opportunities. A powerful person can undulate between possibilities and not get nailed down to someone else's agenda. A powerful person can arrive at a clear intent like a laser. A powerful person grapples well, takes hold of the issues of his life, and "gets down on the mat." A powerful person persists in getting what he wants, through the energy of rolling waves. A powerful person is not afraid to use the whirlwind if it is necessary, but is wise enough and circumspect enough never to use it when it is inappropriate for the circumstances. The Shadow Warrior's motto is "Pray for peace but be prepared for war."

Reminders to Your Warrior Mind

1. *Attentive curiosity* is known as a threshold energy. It is the foundation of all six of the energies. You are open to taking in everything going on around you, where you learn to calmly and clearly observe what is going on in your life. When you can isolate yourself emotionally from circumstances, even for a few seconds, by going into the calm space of attentive curiosity, the energies within you begin

to respond in ways that will alleviate anxiety and allow you to take clear and appropriate action.

2. *Undulation* is a side-to-side motion, a flowing, relaxed swaying. Physically it is one of the most effective self-defense techniques as it can help you release yourself from anyone who has you in a strong grip. Psychologically, it's the process of easily moving from one thought to another and not getting stuck in any one perception. Undulation energy is imaginative, creative, playful, innovative, and re-sourceful.

3. *Clear intent* is knowing exactly what you want and, more importantly, understanding what you want. Clear intent is about moving from the wanting to the intending. The energy of clear intent validates your direction and points your energy toward a focus. It's more than just goal setting. It's the actual process of affirming that in the energy of your mind, you already have what it is you want. It is the energy that helps you manifest concrete results in your life.

4. *Grappling* is taking on a situation, wrestling with it, engaging with it. The best grappling position, either physically or mentally, is from "down on the mat," getting beneath your opponent. When you fight from the ground up, you are using the energies of both your mind and body to defeat whatever it is that's trying to bring you down. This can apply to business situations, relationship conflicts, physical self-defense situations, and mental and spiritual exploration.

5. *Rolling waves* is the energy of targeted persistence, rolling in, rolling out. It's the strategy of moving in, then pulling

back to wait for a response, and moving in again. Rolling waves also helps you combine your energies with another person's, so that negotiation or confrontation or creative brainstorming and action plans go more smoothly and gain more energy. A main principle of many martial arts is the ability to use the "opponent's" own energies to help bring resolution.

6. *The whirlwind* is pulling out all the stops. To use a military analogy, it's a "force multiplier," your own psychological shock and awe. It is explosive, high octane, and "take no prisoners." But it is never out of control. You could use the whirlwind energy to launch a marketing campaign, do battle with a serious illness, or defend yourself when a lot of verbal force (assertiveness) may be needed.

CHAPTER 3

Thinking Like a Shadow Warrior

It all begins in your mind, which filters every reality you experience and perceive. Whether you feel inwardly safe, inwardly confident, and empowered, or insecure, anxious, and powerless, it's first and foremost a state of mind. This is the major premise of the discipline of martial skills: the warrior's state of mind and his understanding and application of that state of mind.

So what then is this mind that can play such tricks on us, and how do we train our mind to be an ally rather than a continual alarm system?

The Nature of the Mind

In our Western culture, when we say "mind" we tend to equate it with thoughts. The field of psychology has widened the concept of the mind to include not only thoughts, but also all the subconscious and unconscious content of the mind, the irrational parts of the mind over which we appear to have no control. In Eastern cultures, "mind" is even vaster: thoughts, feelings, illusions, emotions, touching on the very nature of reality as it melts into the "no-mind" state of nirvana.

I was twenty-five feet down, looking up at the underside of rolling waves in a large body of water. My instructor, who was taking me through a diving requalification course, gave me the instruction for the most basic of things a diver has to do, which is to remove your mask, put it back on filled with water, and then clear it. It was a function I had done thousands of times. But this time my mind decided to act up and say, "No, don't take off the mask! It's too dangerous! You'll die!" I froze. I couldn't take the mask off. This was a totally irrational fear. I knew it was irrational, but nevertheless I gave my instructor the sign that we needed to surface. All my mind was saying was, "You have to get out of here! Go up! Go up!" We went up to the surface, removed our mouthpieces, and I said to him, "I've got a brain lock going on." He said, "Not a problem; it happens to all of us. Let's go through the rest of the exercise and come back to it later."

We went back down. Right at the end of the exercise, he turned to me and gave me the signal to take the mask off. I took it off, put it back on, cleared it, gave him the "thumbs up," and away we went. The point is this: The mind is a very irrational creature. At that moment, it threw fear into me. It brought to my attention my vulnerability. But I had the conditioning and training to introduce both thought and motion as a way to solve my dilemma: I had to get my instructor to come to the surface (motion) so that we could try it all again. Remember: Thought + Motion = No Room for Fear. Thought combined with motion keeps fear at bay. Did the fear go away? No. Could it come back? Of course it could. Do I know how to handle it? Yes, I do.

The field of mind is vast—science is still wrestling with its depth and breadth. My interest in the mind is strictly as it relates to inhibiting you from doing what you want to do. The mind is our seat of consciousness where thinking and feeling take place. The mind involves intellect, reason, understanding, emotions, feelings, the whole of the psyche, and mindfulness.

Being mindful is to condition the mind to think in the here and now. Our mind is chronically restless—it's always in the past or in the future. It's always running off somewhere into the realm of fantasy, or brooding on worries, or daydreaming about how the "grass is greener somewhere else."

Sometimes the experience of being in a totally unfamiliar environment brings us to the energy of mindfulness. For example, you're an urban person living in a city and you've become accustomed to all the background city noise. You decide to take a wilderness camping trip. Out there in the middle of nowhere, you become aware that the "silence" of the forest is very noisy. You hear every single sound and react to it—the crack of a twig, the flapping of a bat's wings, the howl of a wolf. Your sense of hearing has suddenly become very acute. You're so aware of these new sounds that you may not even sleep well. I remember a friend telling me that once on a camping trip her eight-year-old daughter complained, "I couldn't sleep all night, Mommy. The quiet was too loud!"

This phenomenon happens quite naturally. We don't go on the camping trip and consciously think to ourselves, "Okay, I'm going to pull all my senses to the forefront because I'm out in the boonies." You don't have to. Your mind will automatically do it for you. So how come most of the time we appear to have lost our ability to be in the here and now? In our urban-based environments, we have lived so long with so many stimuli that our minds have learned to tune them out.

But since it's the nature of mind to be aware of something, our minds replace the here and now with all the thoughts and fantasies about the past and future. It takes some practice to recover our mindfulness.

The Mind of the Heart and the Heart of the Mind

As I mentioned above, whereas our Western concept of the mind equates it primarily with thoughts and thinking, Eastern philosophies and spiritualities, particularly Buddhism, see mind as encompassing all of human experience. Many people today have taken up the practice of mindfulness meditation. This practice, which comes to us from Buddhist roots, has relevance for all walks of life and blends very well with our traditions and backgrounds, no matter what they are. Every martial art also has a meditative practice attached to it. Laypeople see the martial arts as primarily dealing with bodily self-defense, but these systems are in fact sophisticated spiritual disciplines. Mindfulness, however, can be practiced simply for its own sake and is accessible to anyone.

If you want to have a greater sense of inner safety, inner confidence, balance, and empowerment, it is your total responsibility to cultivate your mind, to guide your mind toward total awareness of where you are and why you're there. Once you are on this path, you will see its benefits. Many people think that meditation means you have to sit and look at a blank wall or be in a monastery. But basically, mindfulness meditation is a simple process of simply sitting, breathing quietly, and watching your thoughts rise and fall in your mind. There is also walking meditation. You can walk in a forest or in your garden or in a park and bring your mind to relaxation by absorbing the sights and smells and the sense of groundedness to the earth. It's all about being completely in the moment.

If you want to do a mindfulness meditative practice, you simply sit quietly in a comfortable position and begin to follow your breath. As you do that, you'll find that all kinds of thoughts and emotions are triggered in your mind. Various emotions may come to the surface and may be bothersome. The idea of meditation is that you're focused on your breathing, observing your thoughts, and observing your emotions rather than fighting with them. Let them come. Let them go. Practice not attaching to your thoughts. When you're uncomfortable with a thought or a feeling and you think, "I don't want to think about that," you are thereby giving power and authority to that thought. In other words, by resisting thoughts, you strengthen them. So instead of doing that, change your perception and focus on your breathing, and let your thoughts and feelings come and go without judgment. Just let them go.

Most of us spend all our time locked in the past or worrying about the future. We carry our past and our hopes for the future with us wherever we go. We carry both the happy and unhappy stuff of our lives. And so if we want a powerful and clear mind that makes us feel centered within ourselves, we need to cultivate a practice of just laying down the thoughts of past and future and "coming home" to the now. Otherwise, the "then" or the "yet to be" dominates our experience and we miss out on what is happening right now. The only moment you truly have is right now. The past is gone. The future hasn't happened yet. I know many spiritual teachers from many traditions say this, and it may be a cliché. But it's a cliché that holds a lot of truth.

For example, I have colleagues who have gone through

very nasty divorces. They wouldn't wish that experience on their worst enemies. They went through it ten years ago, and they just couldn't forget the experience. But eventually they realized that they had to get on with life. They discovered that they didn't have to live that experience day in and day out. I know people who went through the trauma of war many years ago. For some, the memories are as vivid as if it were still happening right now. For others, the memories are something they live with but they don't stop them from living in the now. You don't forget; you *can't* forget. Our minds record and store every experience we have ever had. But you can't allow experiences from "back then" to limit or blind you to the experience of right here, right now.

You can make the choice of whether you want to live perpetually in the pain of past negative experiences. The point is to understand that you don't have to. Is it reasonable to hold one's wife accountable for her actions before you met? It's not helpful to entangle our relationships now with other past relationships. If we do that, we're not giving our partners the courtesy of allowing them just to be themselves without having to carry all the baggage we project onto them. But, you may protest, these are things we do unconsciously. We don't realize we're projecting. It's not intentional! How do we stop doing it? The answer is through cultivating mindfulness.

When you take a break for a period of time each day and calmly observe the flow of your thoughts and feelings, and just let them float on through, you begin to free yourself from both the trappings of the past and the worries and wishes about the future. It really does work. It's a process. And it's something you should do regularly because you gain from the growth you experience. It's not like building a box to put yourself into. It's about dismantling the rigid perceptions in your mind.

The mind loves to sabotage us when we're not expecting it. The mind never ever forgets your experiences, and it will, at the most inappropriate moments, present you with the emotion of those experiences all over again when you don't want it, can't afford it, and have no defense for it. When it comes to energy and the process of our thoughts, our minds do not distinguish between good and bad. Some vulnerability in us, or some association we make in a thought, triggers memories and feelings that seem to come out of nowhere. So maybe you're having a great day—you've just had a success at work—and suddenly you remember the argument you had last week with your spouse, or your kids, or a friend, and your mind has just thrown this giant wet blanket over your feelings of happiness.

You cannot measure a thought. You can't see how long it is or how wide it is. But you can respond to a thought or you can choose not to respond. When you've been doing the practice of observing your thoughts for a time, you begin to see the constant changeability of thoughts. You quietly witness your own thoughts. And you'll find that the thoughts will become just a little less heavy, and you'll get the inklings of a feeling that you are okay exactly the way you are, no matter what you are thinking or feeling. This okayness is what gives you the feeling of inner safety to go through your life.

When they think of the martial art of Ninjitsu, people imagine the Shadow Warrior as one who does things by stealth, a person who can move silently and quickly, even invisibly, in and out of conflict situations. The movie image of the black-clad Ninja leaping on you from the roof when you didn't know he was there is very exciting but is not entirely accurate. Although it's true that Ninjitsu Shadow Warrior training includes such experiences and abilities, the Shadow

Warrior, more importantly, is one who can be aware of and master the unseen parts of life—in other words, the thoughts that go through the mind. We don't see our shadowy thoughts. We see the *results* of thoughts when we take them into action, and if the action is ineffective, it may be too late to retract. The Shadow Warrior will "see" the thought, through her trained awareness, and then decide whether to act on it.

The Six Energies and Your Mind

The next sections explore how you can teach your mind to be receptive to the six energies described in this book.

TEACHING YOUR MIND ATTENTIVE CURIOSITY

In the mind of a Shadow Warrior, there are three main qualities, the triple A's: awakeness, awareness, attentiveness. Let's start with *awakeness*. You know what it's like to walk around with your mind not particularly focused on anything. Your mind has gone on automatic pilot. But the problem is you don't realize you are on automatic pilot, and so you miss seeing the details of where you are. You go through life asleep to your own experiences. So the first thing the Shadow Warrior mind has to do is wake up. Being awake means taking in your surroundings. It's noticing where the trees are, where the road is, and it's also noticing what's going on inside you.

The most important point I can make about the three A's is that they are not separate from each other. They are interconnected. Let's say you walk by an office in your workplace that you've never paid much attention to, and let's say that today you're in *awake* mode, taking in your environment.

Suddenly you become *aware* of something new. An impulse comes in—it's your internal radar, sensing a new energy. You notice a person whom you haven't seen before sitting in that office. Your awakeness has made you aware of something new, and then your *attentiveness*—your reconnaissance—comes in to cause you to focus on the question, "I wonder what that person is doing there?" You can't be aware unless you're awake, and you can't be awake and aware without focusing your attention.

Even sitting down at your own desk, you may start scanning because your mind has picked up on something different. Someone has put a memo on your desk. The important thing to note is that you're actively scanning, not just daydreaming. If you're actively scanning and taking things in, you're awake. Your awakeness triggers your awareness of the memo, and your awareness leads you to the attentiveness of reading the memo. In the human condition, it is natural that people want to go where they are wanted, stay where they feel needed, and grow where they feel comfortable and empowered to grow. The Zenlike paradox is that it's not like planting a seed but it *is* like planting a seed—it is both. The step of attentive curiosity, if it is to function well for you, is based on your love of your own life, not on the love of another person, but of *you*. It is the conviction you have within yourself that it is right to act in your own best interest, for your own well-being, and to be awake and aware to the circumstances that most empower you.

The state of attentive curiosity is when you gather your scattered energies, quiet your mind, enter a situation, and simply observe it without bias and without reaction. It's having the attitude, "I wonder what will happen now. What is this about?" It's an attentive curiosity that not only makes you sharper in terms of being more effective and productive, but also alerts you to possible ambushes. Maybe someone is shaking your hand and saying "good job" but you know that person is a rival for your job and is envious of you. So beware of that handshake. Be attentively curious as to whether there might be a "knife" in the other hand.

Your attentive curiosity allows you to take a look at the changes happening in your life, whether in the course of a day, a week, a month, a year, or more, without becoming upset, without prejudice, without bias. In doing this, you are creating an opportunity to learn why something happened. This is the mind of a Shadow Warrior: to see the unseen. If you allow your feelings and prejudices to run your show, you will not gain the understanding.

It's easy to get emotional about our challenges—about the loss of a relationship, the loss of rank, a conflict with a co-worker or family member. But if your mind is trained to attentive curiosity, it will let the emotion come and go. Never resist an emotion. Let it come and go. Resisting an emotion gives it power. If you give power to a negative emotion, you are conditioning yourself to feel bad. These feelings will hold you back. If you want the heights of life, you have to take a risk, and if your mind is in a state of attentive curiosity, you can feel safer in stretching your parameters to remain comfortable within that risk. If you train your mind into attentive curiosity, you don't cling to things. If something doesn't happen one way for you, some other way will happen.

One of the best ways to teach yourself to use attentive curiosity is to practice some form of mindfulness meditation. Not only will this bring more clarity to your mind; it will also lower your stress. I have described briefly in this chapter how this kind of practice is done. Many books and tapes are available on mindfulness, and there are centers where you can go for instruction. It is very possible, however, to teach yourself.

TEACHING YOUR MIND UNDULATION

When you don't cling to things, when you allow yourself to see that in any situation you have several options, you're moving into mental undulation. You may recall from Chapter 2 that I described undulation as a side-to-side moving-forward energy, similar to how a snake moves. Applied mentally, it's an energy that can get you unstuck. When you have set a goal or a project for yourself, you want to go in that direction. The undulation is how you are going to get there.

The reason to keep the technique of undulation at the forefront of your mind—of continually looking for another way, another perception—is that when you start moving toward your goal, challenges arise and may be significant enough to distract you and prevent you from succeeding. Perhaps someone doesn't believe you can do it and undermines your confidence. Or you feel you have bitten off more than you can chew.

I remember during my military training the first time I fired a submachine gun during target practice and saw the results, I cleared the weapon, set it down, and called my instructor over and said, "I'm not sure I want to do this. I need a moment to think about what I'm doing." I knew on one level that it was part of the training and on another level that handling weaponry entails a huge personal and psychological responsibility. I had to undulate mentally to come to the acceptance that this was an aspect of my duties that I needed to master if I wanted to remain in the military. I had to allow my mind to weave around the discomfort I was feeling, including focusing for a time on other aspects of my training that were less disconcerting, and then returning to target practice with a greater degree of acceptance as to what my responsibilities were.

Mental undulation is also a strategy for dealing with other people's dynamics in getting what you want. In some situations, going straight at something in an "in your face" way may not get you the result you want. If you inappropriately annoy your boss, your commanding officer, or people you are accountable to, that could be a problem. If it's a matter of getting someone to agree to facilitate your goal, if you do it in such a way that you're not rubbing someone's nose in it by taking alternate action, you're more likely to win. You can't just say "up yours" without taking into consideration what that means. People have long memories when it comes to the bad stuff and short memories when it comes to good stuff. Always be aware of potential consequences. Using the energy of undulation is a natural thing to do when you're trying to get people to support circumstances in your favor.

As an example, two long-term staff members left my employ to start their own company in competition with mine, taking several of our key accounts with them. My company was forced into the position of having to protect its customer base. I went directly to the CEOs of several of our accounts and asked for their support. The CEOs assured us that they would continue purchasing from our company. Getting this support was a key step in allowing the company to continue and to recover from this setback. Mental undulation means that instead of being overwhelmed by the anger and disappointment caused by such a situation, I allowed my mind to creatively come up with possible directions and ways of doing damage control. I didn't allow my mind to get stuck in the negative feelings but rather allowed other ideas to flow through and around those feelings, until clarity emerged as to what to do. Visiting the CEOs was one such positive direction.

There are certainly times when direct assertiveness or a "take no prisoners" approach is more appropriate, and we'll be talking about that in terms of some of the other strategies later in the book. Your attentive curiosity and your mental undulation are the tools to help you discern exactly what path you should take, what attitude you should have, and how to get there.

Undulation is an energy of harmony. One of the reasons I was really attracted to Ninjitsu Shadow Warrior training is its emphasis on resolving conflict and living in harmony with your life and with those around you. To bring resolution to conflict, the very first rule of defense, way beyond anything else, is creative thinking. Creative thinking is an expression of undulating energy.

With undulation, the mind can move quickly in a situation through a series of possibilities (Thought + Motion = No Room for Fear). That's what mental undulation really is: It's the process of looking for alternatives, not being stuck on one idea or way of doing things, weaving an energy pattern of new possibilities, thinking outside traditional categories.

Some people think that one way to experience undulation energy is to make lists of pros and cons regarding any problem or situation. But such linear lists force your mind into rigidity. You're too busy trying to make your lists balance. A far more effective strategy for mental undulation is the following "cluster-circular" exercise:

Get a blank piece of paper and put a phrase or key word symbolizing your problem in the center of the paper. Then let your mind free flow. Jot down words or phrases that come to mind in association with the problem. Put the words or phrases anywhere on the paper; it doesn't matter if it looks all jumbled. All you're doing is allowing your mind to undulate all around the page. After doing this for about fifteen minutes, pause and read what you've written. See whether some patterns emerge, whether certain ideas or images cluster on one part of the page or whether they suggest a certain theme.

Mental undulation makes your mind come alive. You can feel very energized from going through a process of creative thinking as you apply it to areas of your life. And the sense of empowerment that comes from knowing you have choices and possibilities makes you feel safer inside yourself because you feel more confident about being who you are. You see yourself as a problem solver or an innovator. You get yourself unstuck. And once you're unstuck, you can then experience the next energy, which is clear intent.

TEACHING YOUR MIND CLEAR INTENT

In the conflict situation I talked about in the Introduction involving the two guys on the dark street, instead of my following their lead, I got them to follow mine. My conduct took their energy away from them. That's a major principle of many martial arts: to blend your energy with your opponent's so that you take your opponent's energy to give yourself an advantage in the conflict. In order to take that energy, you have to have a clear intent to do so. You have to know what your intention is and validate to yourself what it is you are going to do.

Are you focused on what you're going to do or are you focused on doubt? Are you focused on uncertainty or on the steps you can take? Are you focused on someone else's agenda or on what *you* want? When you arrive at your clear intent to do something, when your mind says, "Yes, this is what I'm going to do" and you really mean it, you will have the energy to carry out the action.

During the time I trained in hard-hat diving, one exercise involved stepping down a ladder from the stern of a naval ship used for diver training. At the last rung my head was still above the water. A diving assistant (referred to as a diver's tender) held the other end of my safety rope. Within reach to my left was a hawser (thick rope) tied from the stern of the ship near the ladder. I had to swing over to it in preparation for lowering myself to the bottom.

When you're wearing all that diving gear, you're very heavy (negative buoyancy) and you can't see too well. I remember the mental transition of how it feels going from above the surface of the water to below the surface. Realizing that you are totally counting on someone else for your safety is not the most comforting feeling in the world. You have to learn to trust your tender. I swung over, grabbed the hawser successfully, did my exercise for about forty-five minutes underwater, and then gave the signal that I was coming back up.

Back on the surface, there was another guy preparing to go down for his exercises. He swung over to the hawser but couldn't get his head under the surface of the water. He just couldn't do it. He couldn't get through his fear. He was unable to arrive at the clear intent to go through the exercise because he allowed his mind to spook him. He was given three chances but he still couldn't do it. He had totally lost his intent.

In my own diving exercise, I had walked myself through the steps, stating to myself what I was going to do. I, too, felt anxiety about it, but as soon as I was under the water, I was fine. *You have to get your head under the water.* The secret to doing so, figuratively speaking, of course, is to focus on your breathing. Slow down your breathing, relax, and keep breathing.

The idea of breathing slowly and deeply as a way of calming yourself is a well-known strategy for controlling nervousness in all kinds of situations, such as public speaking, job interviews, making a marriage proposal, or even if you're just feeling irritable about something. Most people have a tendency when anxious to breathe shallowly and more rapidly. By deliberately slowing the pace of your breathing, you influence your physiology to calm down so that you can get a clearer focus and whatever your challenge is won't seem so scary.

If you can breathe, you can do anything. If you stop breathing, if you seize up, you'll never get your head under the water, you'll never get your head into your project, you'll never get into something you need to do. But once you have gotten to your own clear intent, you're already doing it. Once you focus your mind like a laser and say *yes* to what it is you want to do, your mind will validate that intent, and you will feel a sureness, a confidence, despite the fact that you may still be nervous. It's a safe place to be inside yourself when you know that you can empower yourself to do something simply by having a strong intent and not wavering from that clear intent in your mind until you get it done.

TEACHING YOUR MIND TO GRAPPLE

If you're in a situation where you have to give a presentation, or defend yourself from an accusation, or justify yourself, or deal with a conflict, or perform a highly demanding task, it's no good at that point to be wondering how you should be doing it. You should have arrived at that previously by going through attentive curiosity and mental undulation. That's where you ask yourself the "what if" questions. When you get to your clear intent, when you validate the intent of what you're going to do, you get started. You engage. You take it on. You grapple.

Once you get started with something—a task, a process, an interaction—the sequence will fall into place for you. The situation will keep evolving as long as you apply motion to it, as long as you keep giving it life and bringing it into being. Through mental undulation you have cultivated the ability to come at an issue or a circumstance from several different points of your "compass." Grappling is when you get involved with it, when you seize hold of it, when you try this, when you try that, when you stay, when you walk away, when you get closer, when you add to it, when you get on top, when you get underneath.

Some people ask me, "Isn't this the same as undulation?" It can appear very similar. But there is a difference. With undulation, you're holding the main point in your mind, but you're weaving around it. You haven't taken on the issue yet. You're playing with it. With grappling, you take hold. With grappling you're in close quarters, hand to hand with the issue or goal. As you experience this, you will begin to feel the difference between the two energies.

For example, you've signed up for a university course and you have to write a 2,000-word essay. Your professor has given you ten possible topic areas from which to choose. In mental undulation, you'll consider each one, perhaps jumping back and forth between several topics, getting the feel for which topic interests you most or which topic will most reflect your goals in the course, thinking about where you might find the resources, considering what topics the other students may choose, and so forth. That's mental undulation.

Then when you finally decide on your topic, you go to the library and you look up your reference materials. You read what other authors have said about the topic and you begin to formulate your own ideas. You become aware of the viewpoints that you agree or disagree with. Perhaps you even make an appointment to talk with the professor about your topic. Or you meet with other students who are tackling the same topic and trade ideas and critique each other's ideas. Then it's time for you to take a stab at writing a first draft. You revise and edit and rearrange, and maybe even feel like you want to pull your hair out, but you go back to it anyway and rewrite some more until you have a final version that you hand in to your professor. That's mental grappling.

The secret to good grappling is to hold an empty mind. Even in this process of "engaging with the enemy"—whether the "enemy" is a paper you need to write, a boss you ask for a raise, a difficult argument with your spouse, or the effort to learn a new skill—even in the midst of all this grappling, you sense the still center of your mind. You engage with your issue but you don't attach to it. You maintain your balance.

Mental grappling helps you release the inhibitors in your mind. When you're in the flow of the grappling energy, your mind will give you what you need. It's there. If you put a blocker in your mind, if you give in to doubt or uncertainty, you're basically putting grappling hooks on your mind, tying it up.

It's not the grappling hooks you need, but the *grappling itself*. If you remove the blocks, even just a bit at a time through your grappling, the mind will be freed up to give you creative expression.

Keep focused on your breathing and welcome the emotion of the experience, whatever it is. This takes practice. You are the one who must grapple with your own issues and goals. Part of the problem is that we often want to give others the job of grappling, to have it done for us, and then we're surprised at being unhappy with the result. People often say to me, "I want to get involved with martial arts, so which school or type of practice would you recommend?" And I always say, "None of them—because the experience has to be all yours." You have to go through phone books and go to the various schools and find in your heart where you make a connection. Find where the energy is for you that will open your mind. You need to grapple, to take it on, to try it for yourself, not just follow along on someone else's recommendation.

When you find something for yourself, when the truth you arrive at in a situation is your own truth, your own valid experience, you will find that your energy becomes natural and free. As you practice mental grappling in your life, it will eventually become instinctual.

TEACHING YOUR MIND ROLLING WAVES

Rolling waves in the mind is an energy that helps bring you to the resolution phase of dealing with challenges. The image of rolling waves in the ocean suggests two things—first, an ebb and a flow, and second, an energy of targeted persistence.

Consider *ebb and flow*. The ocean just keeps washing up against that shore, over and over. Applying a mental rolling wave to a situation can involve changing habits, chipping away at how you've always done things, and through continual practice—continual "waves"—you change your mind regarding that habit, and in that way you change your behavior. You throw a rolling wave at a circumstance, and everything begins shifting to accommodate your intent.

Now consider *targeted persistence*. Rolling waves are the energy that guides you to keep at something, to be relentless in what you want, but also to be gentle. A typhoon is not a rolling wave. It's a crashing wave. Don't be a typhoon; just be a wave. The rolling wave carries with it the aspect of pulling back and observing. You move into a situation and then you pull back for a while to see what happens.

One example of rolling wave energy is when you're putting in an offer on a house. You see a house you like. You can't quite afford it, but you really want it. So you make an offer. That's a wave. The seller comes back with a counteroffer or more conditions. You pull back, regroup, and then throw another wave, making your offer again in a modified form.

At this point, both buyer and seller are throwing waves. Eventually there will be a resolution. Hopefully you will get your house, but even if you don't, you will have gained confidence in the sureness of how you held your position and went through the process. And chances are, if you have a quiet, calm mind and use your attentive curiosity to observe the situation fully—where the strengths are, where the weaknesses are—you have already used mental undulation by looking at various types of houses so that you now know what you want. If you have arrived at your clear intent that this is the kind of house you want, and if you have grappled with yourself (and also with your bank) as to how you can arrange the financing, chances are that after all that, your waves are going to be more effective than the seller's. Most people don't stand a chance in the presence of a good grappler and good wave thrower who knows what she wants.

Many people interrupt the flow of their own rolling waves by talking too soon after they have thrown their wave. The silences while you wait for a response are as important as the wave itself. The next time you make a suggestion to someone (throw a wave), then pause and settle. Await the person's response with calmness and attentive curiosity. Don't jump in and try to answer it for the person or make helpful suggestions. Don't block that person's wave. Wait to see what the response will be to *your* wave. We'll be talking more about this in later chapters when we look at examples of how this works in the job environment and in relationships.

In the mind, rolling waves are the energy of determination. But it's not a stubborn determination; it's a flowing determination. It's the determination of going after what you want, but still not attaching to what you want. The ocean does not attach to the shore. It just keeps touching the shore. And which is the more powerful? The water that relentlessly and steadily washes the shore, or the solidity of the shoreline? Of the four natural elements—earth, air, fire, and water—water is the softest but it is the mightiest. That's why so often you hear martial arts teachers tell their students, "Be like the water."

TEACHING YOUR MIND THE WHIRLWIND

In the mind, the whirlwind is a final thrust of energy that totally blows away any inner resistance. When you get that little voice inside your head that says, "You shouldn't do this, you shouldn't do that," and you get to the point where you say, "*Shut up!*" to those thoughts, that's the intention of the whirlwind to overcome all resistance, internal and external. Don't be ruled by the negative tendencies of your mind. Find them, bring them out in the open, and boot their asses out the door. You can destroy your inner enemy of doubt, uncertainty, and anxiety with the pure force of your intention and your will.

"Wait a minute," you may be thinking, "didn't he just tell us earlier in the chapter that we're not supposed to resist thoughts?" Yes, I did say that. And there's a subtlety here that sometimes is difficult to grasp. There is a difference between resisting thoughts and overcoming thoughts. The practice of observing your thoughts and just letting them flow through without reacting to them eventually results in an increase in your awareness of your thoughts. Once you have cultivated the awareness of the thoughts without attaching to them, you are now in a position to overcome or stop those thoughts you do not desire.

Overcoming a thought doesn't happen from a place of attachment and resistance. It happens from a place of clear intent as to whether or not that thought serves you at that point in time. In the midst of a meditative practice, it's not necessary to take that kind of "mind action" of the whirlwind. What I'm talking about is what you do with negative thoughts when they affect you in concrete situations involving actions and decisions. If you have cultivated nonresistance to thoughts, the negative thoughts reveal themselves much more quickly and your awareness of them is also clearer, so at that point you can choose to unleash the whirlwind and say no to any thoughts that creep into the situation to undermine you.

This doesn't happen overnight. In fact, you have implemented the whirlwind by your very understanding that it's not a quick-fix process. Your willingness to work with and feel your own energies and harness them into supporting your life and meeting your challenges releases the whirlwind.

You may think you've overcome something. You may feel

that you have finally silenced the objections within. But, lo and behold, the old doubts and fears come out when you're emotionally tired or spiritually tired, or when you've had a negative experience in your life, and you find yourself besieged by your mind telling you everything you've done wrong, stirring up worries, making you brood on what ifs. You say to those doubts, "Wait a minute. I thought I had killed you." And the mind says, "Uh-uh! Not a chance." And you say to yourself, "Okay, so I didn't kill you, but I can kick you out of the way!" The beauty is that once you've kicked your doubts and fears once, using the whirlwind, the next time is much easier. Those doubts then only have half their strength to bear on you. And you kick them again, and they only have a third of their strength. You can't entirely get rid of the "bad guys" in your psyche—the fears, doubts, uncertainties, worries, and conflicts—but by connecting to the energy of the whirlwind, you can diminish their impact on you when they are affecting you at times when you need your mind to be clear, positive, and focused.

Most often, the energies of attentive curiosity, undulation, clear intent, grappling, and rolling waves are enough to get you where you want to go. Often it's not necessary to resort to the whirlwind to smack those fears and doubts inside you "upside the head."

Clear Mind, Powerful Mind

We've seen how the six energy moves are reflected at the mental level, which is where everything begins. If you want to change how you act and the results you get, you have to change how you think. More important, you have to alter the energies inside you and around you and use your mind to do it. As you learn to mix and match these energy forces, your mind gets clearer. In the martial arts we say that a clear mind is a powerful mind. And a powerful mind leads to powerful actions.

When it comes to personal change, fear will always be there even if it's not always recognizable. It's a fact of life. Risk is something we accept for the privilege of just being alive. If mentally you accept the risk, and you resolve to go forward anyway with your life, what's the problem? The problem is that you're still sitting there thinking about it. Now get your ass moving!

In the chapters that follow, we're going to look at how you can learn and experience the energies of each of the six moves in many different areas of your life.

Reminders to Your Warrior Mind

1. In our Western culture, we equate mind solely with thoughts and thinking. In Eastern cultures, mind is a much vaster concept—encompassing thoughts, feelings, illusions, emotions, touching on the very nature of reality.

2. The best way to train your mind to be receptive to the six energies and how they work in your life is to practice mindfulness meditation. Many people think meditation has to take up a lot of time or that it's too esoteric, but a mindfulness practice is actually very simple. You simply sit quietly and follow your breathing, watching the thoughts rise and fall in your mind without attaching to them. It is all about being present in the moment.

3. The mind of a Shadow Warrior is a mind that can see the unseen, that is, thoughts. Many of us go through a day thinking all kinds of thoughts without even being aware that those thoughts are there as background noise, trapping us in the past or projecting us into the future. The mind of the Shadow Warrior follows the three A's: awakeness, awareness, attentiveness.

4. Mindfulness is the key to attentive curiosity, the gathering of scattered energies, entering a situation and simply observing it. When you do not cling to your thoughts, you find that your thoughts begin to undulate. You begin to see possibilities, consider alternatives. Undulation is not making lists of goals. It's more of a free-flow brainstorming. Practice the "cluster-circular" undulation exercise in this chapter.

5. Are you focused on what you're intending to do or are you focused on doubt? Are you focused on someone else's agenda or on your own? Clear intent is when your mind says, "Yes, this is what I am going to do." When you grapple mentally with an issue, you take it on. A situation will keep evolving as long as you apply motion to it: *Thought + Motion = No Room for Fear.*

6. Consider the ebb and flow of your thoughts. Then apply that ebb and flow to your goals and intentions using the energy of rolling waves. Learn to stay out of the way of your own rolling waves by not interrupting the energy too soon. Make use of strategic silence. And if you need to access the whirlwind, use it to destroy the inner enemy of doubt, uncertainty, and anxiety with the pure force of your intention, your creativity, and your will.

CHAPTER 4

Handling Daily Challenges

You are leaving your house on a gray Monday morning to go to work. Now what can go wrong besides earthquakes, floods, or fire? A lot of little things. You notice that your car has a flat tire. Damn, that slow leak stopped being a slow leak. Now you're going to be late.

You change your tire and drive to work on the doughnut tire, making a mental note that you have to stop on the way back from work to get a proper tire put on. Now you notice that your gas gauge is virtually on empty. Your teenage son drove the car all over town on the weekend and didn't bother refilling the tank. You pull in for gas, and all you can think about is what your boss is going to say when you miss a priority meeting that was set for the beginning of the week.

When you get to work your designated parking spot has been taken by someone else. So you drive around and around trying to find another spot, cursing the owner of the interloper car, ending up at the far end of the parking lot. Naturally, it has started to rain. You step out of your car and lock your keys inside. You had laid them on the seat while you fumbled for the umbrella you keep in the backseat. Now you're going to have to spend your lunch hour waiting for your road service provider to come out there and help you break into your own car.

What are the emotions involved in hassles like these? Annoyance, irritability, anxiety, anger, and fear. Fear? Yes, fear of having to justify to your whole work team and your boss why you're late. Fear that just when you thought your life was under control with your great job, something as innocent as a flat tire and keys left on the seat could put you in a bad light and make you look inadequate and disorganized.

Here's another daily life hassle situation. You're going to your local hardware store to buy a wrench that you need to repair your garage door. You already have two wrenches but when you started the task this morning, you found that neither of them was the right length or weight. One hardware store doesn't have the kind you need, so you try another, and another—until you've gone halfway across town in search of that elusive perfect tool. You left at 9 A.M. and it's now 11 A.M.

Driving home, you remember that your wife asked you to pick up a few groceries on your way back. So now you have to go get that pound of butter, a dozen eggs, bread, and milk, and you end up contending with long lineups at what is supposed to be the "express checkout." It's now past noon. You have your wrench and your groceries, but half the day has gone by and you haven't started the repairs.

The emotions here? Annoyance, disgruntlement, frustration.

The Challenges of Daily Life

The annoying hassles of life are a reminder that the energies of life will not be contained by our routines and expectations. As the comedian Woody Allen said, adapting a Yiddish proverb, "Want to make God laugh? Tell Him your plans."

YOU KNOW THE ROUTINE

What do we mean when we use the phrase "daily life"? Usually we're talking about the times when our life feels ordinary, when everything, both the good and the bad, moves along more or less the way we expect. We count both our little triumphs and our niggling hassles as daily life. Somehow it feels different from the times when we perceive something big as happening, such as getting married, a loved one dying, losing our job, getting a big promotion, and changing careers. We'll be looking at the six moves and big life events in the next two chapters. In this chapter we're talking about the everyday challenges.

Some people see daily life as everything that happens between the milestones of our lives. Some of us see daily life as meaning Monday to Friday, and not including weekends (or days off if your work schedule sometimes involves weekends). We see our daily life as composed of having the discipline of getting up and going to work, or raising our kids, or going to school, or working in our gardens, or shoveling snow, or doing an exercise routine. No matter the life stage we are in—from youthful student to senior in retirement—daily life is what we come to perceive as what is expected each day.

However, if we dig beneath the surface of our seeming routines, we find an energy current that at any time can make our lives anything but routine. Our precious routines are often buffeted by life and if it were not so, think of how boring life would be. If everything were always the same, you wouldn't grow; you wouldn't change. Daily life routines are wonderful—they get us through the days and weeks—but they can also hide from us the unique learning opportunities present in each and every day, opportunities when we can experience how to keep ourselves in a current of empowerment and moving away from chronic anxiety.

But we are creatures of habit. We want life to be predictable. Very often our concept of daily life is a defense against the feelings of anxiety and hassles that disrupt our lives. We don't want to admit to ourselves that sometimes our lives have an uneasiness to them or that we feel ill equipped to deal with hassles. We don't want to admit that many of us, in the words of Henry David Thoreau, live "lives of quiet desperation." Often we feel we have lost touch with vitality—that's the price we pay for wanting to have everything be predictable and hassle free.

Whether we like it or not, the universe doesn't always cooperate. Hassles and disruptions to our daily life appear all the time. And if we've lost touch with the energies in our lives—energies that help carry us through challenges, energies that help us handle challenges—our response to the challenges will be full of anxiety and stress.

The challenge is how to cope with daily hassles without having those hassles rob us of joy; how to maintain equilibrium so that we can savor life rather than just endure it.

The first thing to accept is that you cannot protect yourself from circumstances beyond your control. You can't protect yourself from the flat tire you found on your car or from the long lineups in stores or banks. Unless you put the nail there yourself in the driveway or deliberately chose a time when you knew the lineups would be long, the external circumstances are not your responsibility. What *is* your responsibility is how you respond. If other people are depending on you in a certain time frame and you're delayed by unforeseen circumstances, it's your responsibility to inform them of the situation. But you are not responsible for how other people *interpret* your challenge. If someone says, "Well, that's not an acceptable reason for being late," or "We were really counting on you to be here by 9 A.M.; now everything is messed up," it should not change your own relationship to the challenge. Part of using the mind of the Shadow Warrior is to learn not to take on other people's stuff. You have enough to do dealing with your own.

The tendency is for you to think, "Oh dear, they're going to be so upset with me because I'm late," and start getting concerned about someone else's response to your predicament. As a result, the fullness of your attention (the energy of attentive curiosity) is not on solving your challenge but on placating the other person.

DOING EVERYTHING YOU CAN DO

Recently I was driving to another city with my wife to attend the birthday party of a friend. But we soon became aware that we had miscalculated the time it would require to get there, and we were going to be late. So we called our friends from our cell phone and left a message that we would be delayed. At that point, we had done everything we could do to communicate that we were running late. The point is that my wife and I, in traveling to the party, had a zero anxiety level once we had done everything we could possibly do to communicate our impending lateness.

By paying attention to what you can do in any situation, especially in circumstances beyond your control or as a result of a human mistake (such as miscalculating travel time), the mind can remain unencumbered by anxiety.

> Let's look at another example of an annoying hassle that could have wrecked my day if I had allowed it to. One Saturday morning I was pulling into the parking lot of a large mall. I was driving a big three-quarter-ton pickup truck at the time. I wanted to back into the space up against the curb, not out in the center of the parking lot. But wouldn't you know it? As I pulled out to back in, a little car darted into that very space. Now, who among us would not be tempted to get into a bit of a snit about that?
>
> I saw a young man and two young women in the car, laughing and talking and paying no attention to what was going on around them. I really wanted to tear a strip off these people.
>
> I put my truck in park and got out, but by the time I had reached their car, I stopped myself and thought, "I can't do this. Maybe it was not that young man's intent to grab the space out from under me. Insulting him will only cause a negative energy and for what?" So I got back into the truck, found a parking space, and took some deep breaths.
>
> As I walked into the mall, I met up with the young man and his female companions at the door. He said, "Hey, man, I'm so sorry. I really didn't see you sitting there."
>
> I was glad that I had taken the deep breaths, and that I had avoided the psychological violence of making people feel bad about themselves or, for that matter, the psychological violence against myself by getting all

worked up over nothing. I mean, even if the young man had intended to scoop the space, what would have been accomplished by getting all huffy about it? A big part of the mind of a Shadow Warrior is that if you're going to do battle, pick your battles. Save your "troops" for the really important conflicts, where winning will really make a difference.

You can choose a strategy of useless combat or you can employ the skills and mind-set of a peacemaker. The young man chose to be a peacemaker by apologizing. I chose to be a peacemaker by having decided just to let it pass. Some things are just not worth getting anxious or angry about.

ANXIETY AND ANGER

You could look at anger as a relief valve for anxiety. So unless you become aware of what is going on inside you at these times, you can easily go very quickly from anxiety to anger and then to the expression of anger. It's not healthy to keep that stuff all bottled up and pretend it's not there. It's equally not healthy to go around acting it out willy-nilly. It *is* healthy to:

- Gain awareness of the feeling

- Accept the feeling

- Just let it be there

- Choose not to act on it *unless* there is a clear reason for you to do so

As a society we are full of anxiety. It pervades our daily life. We're afraid of violence, terrorism, unemployment, illness. But in the more micro areas of our daily lives, we feel various anxieties about how we are going to be perceived by our peers, by people who work with us, our bosses, our competitors, our neighbors, even by our own intimate loved ones.

We forget that the anxieties we feel are the same anxieties other people are feeling. The reasons for the anxiety can be completely different but the feeling is the same. Using the mind of a Shadow Warrior by going into the mind state of attentive curiosity, you begin to notice the commonality of feelings you share with many people.

RECOGNIZING DANGER

Here's a major advantage of attentive curiosity toward your own mind state and feelings and toward others' mind states and feelings: You learn—gradually—to hone your instincts to know when you really *are* in danger.

When Ninjitsu students asked Grand Master Masaaki Hatsumi, "How do you know you're in danger when you're in a crowd of people?" he would answer, "Your instincts will tell you. And if there is a threat, your instincts will tell you where it's coming from."

However, when we allow our minds to run off into all sorts of extraneous anxieties and hassles, we lose touch with our instincts. As you develop the habit of a clear mind, your instincts will alert you to what's going on before you're in the thick of it, whether the threat is that you're potentially at the wrong end of a gun, or if the "threat" is that your market share is about to take a dive, or if the "threat" is that your boss is in a foul mood this morning and is just hunting in the office for someone to take it out on. Then you'll have the opportunity to undulate mentally around whatever the threat is and not get entangled with the anxieties it provokes.

UNDERSTANDING INSTINCT

Understanding and using instinct—the instinct that comes from being awake, aware, and attentive—is not filtered through a social consciousness. It's not a matter of learning social cues. The instinctive part of you doesn't pay any attention to any of that stuff. Instead, it reads the energies in a situation. Aware instinct is one of the survival tools of both the body and the spirit.

I remember a story of a soldier who was on night patrol in an enemy-controlled area. He was in a ravine with his head above the ravine's edge and something inside him told him to duck. As he did, a round from an AK-47 went right over his head. Then all hell broke loose. Instinct saved his life.

Here's a more mundane example. I was driving up to an intersection, coming to a stop. There was black ice on the road and I began slipping into the intersection against the red light and there was a truck coming straight at me. I really didn't want to become part of that truck's grille. I got my foot off the brake and directed the front wheel onto the gravel, which was not as icy. I managed to make a ninety-degree turn onto the shoulder as the truck went whipping by me. My instinct took over to protect me. Your instinct will never fail you if you understand it and are open to it. Don't block it.

In working with women who have gone through sexual assault, I remember talking with several who had been assaulted by men they thought they could trust, men who were known to them. I asked these women how this circumstance had occurred in their lives. The number one thing that came out was that their instinct was talking to them but their mind-set was such that they were not paying any attention to it. They would think things like:

- "Oh, he looks like such a nice guy."

- "He could never do something like that."

- "But I love him."

All along, their instincts were telling them to beware of something about the guy. Many of the women told me that in hindsight they could see the warning signs but that something had "blinded" them to these cues at the time.

This does not excuse the crimes committed against these women, but it is a wake-up call about why it's necessary to heed our instincts. Some people call this "listening to intuition." But for a Shadow Warrior, it's more primal than intuition; it's instinct.

When the awareness of your mind reaches a stillness and the wisdom of your instincts comes to the surface, you've found an equilibrium that can carry you through your daily life and quell your knee-jerk response to all the anxieties, hassles, and fears that present themselves. The secret of the Shadow Warrior is in the energies—the six energy moves.

Applying the Six Energies to Daily Life

Now we'll look at some situations where the six energies—attentive curiosity, undulation, clear intent, grappling, rolling waves, and the whirlwind—come more clearly into focus.

ATTENTIVE CURIOSITY

Let's go back to the flat tire. Your fallback position in any situation causing you a challenge, large or small, is always to *attentive curiosity*. Always. It takes practice. Your practice of cultivating the calm mind of attentive curiosity toward the reality confronting you is based on not giving in to the perception of "Oh, no, this is really messing me up! Damn car! Damn tire! Damn Monday morning!"

Instead, using attentive curiosity, you say to yourself, "You know, I didn't plan on this happening to me this morning, but I acknowledge that there are always things I can't plan on. So this tire has to be fixed and I have to telephone some folks to let them know I'll be late."

After doing that you confront the tire again. "Now what do I need to do to get the tire fixed? Get out the jack and do it myself? Call the AAA? Get my spouse or a neighbor to help?" Paying attention with a playful curiosity about what is before you is the key to getting to a place of inner calm and security.

UNDULATION

We get into a calm state by consciously addressing the things that are causing the anxiety. Let's imagine a variation on our tire story. Let's say that the flat tire is going to make you late for a presentation in front of 300 people in an auditorium and you don't have time to fix it right now. That's a really good reason to feel anxious. But it is not a reason to let the anxiety lock you up.

This is where you can move into the energy of *undulation*, which will flow very naturally from your attentive curiosity. You look at the possibilities for solving your problem. "Okay,

I need a lift and I need it right now. I could call a taxi. I could call a friend to pick me up. I could catch a bus that comes in ten minutes." That's a mind that is undulating away from negative anxiety toward an energy of resolution.

CLEAR INTENT

Then you come to the energy of *clear intent*. You decide upon the correct path right here, right now, for *this* situation. Never mind all the other times you've had a flat tire. Never mind what you would do with a flat tire on the weekend or after supper or on vacation. Decide what you will do right now in this set of circumstances. "This is the path I'm taking. I'm calling a taxi and I'm getting to the presentation right now, and the AAA can come out and fix the tire later."

Okay, let's get off the flat tire and look at how some of the other energies can be used in daily life situations. Remember that you may not need to call upon all the moves for every situation. In time, your instincts will develop to let you know which ones you need.

GRAPPLING

You've got three weeks of vacation time and you're planning a road trip with your spouse, the kids, and the family dog. With attentive curiosity you've explored some possibilities. You have chosen some possible favorite sites to visit and you and your family have undulated around the possibilities. You arrive at a clear intent that your trip will take you from Connecticut to sunny California. You're going to do it by driving.

Here is where *grappling* comes in. Remember, grappling is

when you take the issue on, when you actually "wrestle" with the details. It's different from undulation because after you've got clear intent, your energy is grappling with *specific* details, not just *possible* details.

So, for example, you need to grapple with the details of the car, for it's the car that's going to carry you all the way to California. What do you need to know about your vehicle before leaving? You need to get the car serviced; you need to know where service centers are along the way for your brand of car; you need to stock the car with a cooler full of drinks and snacks and maybe games. You're grappling with the "putting into action" of your trip. After you grapple about the car, you grapple about the hotels or campgrounds. You grapple about how to keep the kids from killing each other in the back seat or about how often you will need to stop for a pee break for both humans and dog. You've got a list of what you need to know. Knowledge is power. You take control of your own trip, not somebody else's idea of what you should be doing.

ROLLING WAVES

The energy of *rolling waves* can serve us well in situations like this. A friend of mine, Greg, had a landscaping business and his truck needed repairing. He got a quote of $2,000 for the repair, but the bill ended up being $6,000. The repair staff figured they could easily get $6,000 out of the guy because he was a young man in a start-up business and really needed his truck.

Greg and I chatted about what to do. I taught him about *rolling waves*. We scripted the whole thing out, and he followed it to the letter.

The first wave he threw at the truck repair business was a

"no." He told the staff that their pricing was unacceptable. This took them aback, but they still had his truck.

"Here is the money we agreed to," he said, throwing his second rolling wave. "Take it or I will have to consult some authorities."

They thought he was bluffing, so he pocketed the money and left.

The next day he threw a third rolling wave by showing up with a member of the Better Business Bureau. The manager of the repair shop, thoroughly nonplussed, gave Greg back his truck, accepting a check for $2,000.

If Greg had panicked and allowed himself to be intimidated, it would have cost him another $4,000. Instead, he simply stated the path he was on, doing it in waves, not giving them all the information all at once. When they saw that he was not going to back off, that the next wave would be coming at them, *they* backed off. They also developed a new respect for this young man's resolve.

The important thing was that Greg did not act in a hostile fashion. He did not invite them to fight with him. He simply threw his rolling waves and waited for the waves to recede to see what would happen, and then threw another one, calmly, resolutely, not feeling anxious, but rather very much in control of the energies of the situation. He blended his energy with theirs and turned the situation to his favor—a classic move of all martial arts. Needless to say, with targeted persistence like that, today he has a very successful landscape business and a well-repaired truck!

THE WHIRLWIND

The whirlwind is not an energy you are likely going to need a lot in daily life. It's pretty drastic. It's an all-out onslaught on a problem or a situation. If you use the whirlwind energy in an overkill way, you'll become known, even if you're right, as a person who overreacts.

Greg could have used a whirlwind strategy. He might have decided to have the repair company investigated for inflating its prices. This could have led to charges and the closing down of the repair shop. But he got what he wanted before getting to the whirlwind stage. It was not necessary to go the whole distance and really make trouble for the repair shop.

There are some situations when you really do need to go to that kind of distance, but this was not one of them. If it happened to him again with the same company, then, yes, the company would have been courting the whirlwind. But a Shadow Warrior will always choose his or her battles. By choosing your battles wisely, you deal with your situations from an inner position of security and lack of fear.

Strategies to Lessen Daily Anxiety

What is the very bedrock of your life as you experience it from day to day? What is the common denominator between each day and yourself? You. You are the common denominator, the you who lives inside your body.

One way we make ourselves easy prey for day-to-day hassles is by neglecting our bodies. Part of the wisdom carried by every accomplished martial artist is that the care of the body is as important as the discipline of the mind. When you watch a martial artist, or indeed any accomplished athlete, what do you see? You see a person who is healthy and fit.

I am not suggesting that you need to become an athlete or reach the fitness level of a black belt Judoka or Ninjitsu practitioner. What I am suggesting is that if you truly want to be able to access the six energies for your life and make them work for you in your life, you have to take care of yourself. Let's look at the major ways of taking care of ourselves.

EXERCISE

First, there is exercise. Virtually every day a major newspaper somewhere publishes an article about how Western civilization is experiencing an epidemic of obesity. Sedentary lifestyles are increasingly the norm. One recent study actually predicted that the generation of children coming up behind us will have a lower life expectancy than their parents because of the huge increase in childhood obesity.

Your body was made for movement. Your body feels good when it gets to move. You don't have to be an exercise freak in order to add physical activity into your life. David Patchell-Evans, one of the most successful fitness experts in the world and owner of a large chain of fitness clubs, often uses the phrase "good enough is good enough." By that he means that if you can find enough time to include just moderate physical activity in your life, you'll achieve a good level of fitness. You don't have to train for hours like an Olympic athlete. Patchell-Evans teaches his fitness club members that if you find time to exercise half an hour three times a week, and if your exercise routine incorporates both cardiovascular and strength-training exercises, you can reach 95 percent of your maximal fitness in six months.

Numerous studies show that exercise elevates mood and makes people less irritable. It also elevates energy. So exercise can indeed be a very effective way of immunizing yourself against reacting to the hassles of daily life. Exercise can also help you cope with really big challenges by giving you more endurance. Exercise releases endorphins into your body, making you feel good.

There are many ways to incorporate physical activity into your daily life. Walking is one of the most effective types of exercise. It is easy and available and doesn't cost anything. You can enjoy hiking or canoeing or climbing. You can join a fitness club and make use of state-of-the-art equipment. You can join group fitness classes and make exercise a social experience. You can get some exercise tubing and a balance ball and use them in your own home. You can participate in a favorite recreational sport. You can learn a martial art. No matter what your lifestyle is, there are ways you can find to include physical exercise.

NUTRITION

A second way to take care of our bodies is through the food we eat. I'm sure you've heard the expression "you are what you eat." So many of us have a fast-paced and busy lifestyle, trying to juggle career, family, and community involvements, that we often find ourselves hard pressed to find time to eat a nutritious meal. Instead we indulge ourselves in fast food eaten on the fly. The love affair with fast food is a major contributor to the obesity epidemic referred to above. It's interesting that many of the fast-food chains are now offering more nutritious choices such as salads and low-fat entrees. So if you have to avail yourself of a fast-food "fix," include some of the more healthful menu choices.

Some nutritionists point out that it's not only the fact that we don't include enough healthy foods in our diets but that we also eat at such irregular intervals that we confuse our body's metabolism. We skip breakfast, for example, and maybe lunch too if we're really busy, and grab a sandwich in late afternoon. Then we get home from work and pour ourselves a drink. We're not hungry because we ate "lunch" so late, so dinner is put off until later as well. Then we don't sleep well because our stomach is busy digesting the dinner we ate at 10 P.M., which we should have eaten at 6 P.M. It's no surprise that our energy levels go up and down like a roller coaster, making the daily hassles of life that much more difficult to handle.

We all know what a healthy diet is: lots of fruit and vegetables, complex carbohydrates, and a daily allowance of protein. Many nutritionists recommend a complement of dairy products as well, but there are some people who are lactose intolerant and so need to find other dietary sources for calcium.

We also all know what a healthy diet is *not*. It's not French fries, it's not a greasy hamburger, it's not doughnuts, it's not chips, it's not soft drinks.

I'm not going to go into great detail about how to design a healthy, nutritious diet for yourself. There are numerous great books on that topic and numerous community resources that can help you access information on healthful eating. But I do want to emphasize that healthy eating is important and to urge you, as part of the discipline of the six energies, to put into your body foods that are nourishing and healthful. Like exercise, nutritious eating makes you more energetic and better able to withstand stress.

SLEEP PATTERNS

A third way to take care of our bodies is to get enough sleep. Several books and multiple studies in the past few years have identified that our society is sleep deprived. Experts cite technological innovations, such as computers, e-mail, or cell phones, as contributing to the idea that we are on call twenty-four hours a day. Shift work is another factor, as are such phenomena as frequent business travel, which messes up our body's sense of time zones, and the current focus on "lean" workplaces, which means that there are fewer people to do more and more of the work.

So we find ourselves cutting back on sleep. Sure, it's possible to do a few all-nighters and get away with it. But if you keep it up, your body begins to pay the price. Sleep researchers estimate that most people need seven to eight hours of continuous sleep every twenty-four-hour period. Some people need a little less and some people need more. But there are myriad individuals who are trying to get by on only three to four hours of sleep, and research indicates that that is clearly not enough.

Chronic sleep deprivation makes you less alert. It affects your judgment. It compromises your immune system. And it distorts your perceptions. How many of us have reacted to situations with greater anger or irritability than normal because we were tired, situations that would not have bothered us at all if we were feeling alert and rested?

A side effect of sleep deprivation is the huge market in pharmaceutical sleep aids, everything from over-the-counter medications to prescription drugs, all aimed at shutting down our overworked, overstressed brains so that we can get some sleep. The problem is that many of these medications interfere with the most important part of your sleep cycle, the rapid eye movement patterns. If you don't get enough REM sleep, your sleep will not be restorative. So drugs are not the answer.

Physical exercise can help with sleep patterns. New exercisers often report that their sleep has improved. Other things that can help are to avoid caffeine, especially in the evening hours, and not to have television in your bedroom. When it is time to sleep, you don't want to have any kind of stimulus around to keep you awake (unless it is the stimulus of making love with your partner—good sex can do wonders for improving sleep patterns!).

~

You need to look with attentive curiosity at these three areas of your life—your physical activity, your nutrition, and your sleep patterns—and notice where you are out of balance. Then you need to undulate around all the possibilities. Should you be a home exerciser or join a fitness club? Should you order a salad and a fresh fruit cup during lunch or pack yourself a nutritious lunch of your own? Should you decide to give yourself a regular bedtime or should you structure in some time for power naps during your days? There are numerous possibilities open to you that will help you incorporate fitness, healthy eating, and restful sleep into your life.

When you've come up with what will work for you, then make it your clear intent to carry it out. Have a clear intent to devote that half hour three times a week to fitness. Have a clear intent to include more fresh vegetables and fruit in your diet. Have a clear intent to go to bed an hour earlier if you've been sleep depriving yourself.

Don't focus on what you *won't* do. Focus on what you *will* do. In other words, don't tell yourself, "I will not eat doughnuts," because that very thought seeds "doughnuts" in your head and you're going to crave them with a passion. Instead, tell yourself, "I'm going to eat a fresh fruit cocktail with succulent strawberries and juicy cantaloupe," and seed the idea of sweet-tasting fruits in your mind.

Keeping your promises to yourself about more healthful living will require some grappling, to be sure. It's so easy to slip back into old habits. So when you find yourself doing that, take it on, take hold of the promise you made to yourself, and get back "on the mat" with your nutrition plan, your fitness, and your sleep patterns.

As you balance fitness, nutrition, and sleeping patterns in your life, you'll become more conscious of the flowing waves of your daily energies. Make this rolling waves pattern work for you. When you wake up in the morning, the rolling wave of a good breakfast sends you on your way. At lunchtime, another rolling wave arrives in the form of a nutritious lunch. Perhaps on the way home from work, you ride with another wave of going to the fitness club for a workout, followed by the rolling wave of dinner. And then, at night, you calm the sea—you sleep. Have you ever seen a body of water absolutely still in the moonlight, with no motion, just glittering like smooth glass? That's the way your mind should be as it drifts into sleep.

And, finally, if you do the things necessary to balance your body's health, you'll experience a whirlwind of new energy and new vitality. You'll begin to feel like a new person. And that openness to becoming a new and continually evolving person can invite the whirlwind in a good way into your daily life to transform it. That kind of openness can make us receptive to those other whirlwind moments that enter our daily lives and create a fabric of meaning we had never experienced before.

Sometimes the whirlwind can appear to overtake us in our daily lives. This is not always a bad thing. Sometimes it's the energy of the whirlwind entering our daily life that changes the entire way we look at the world. Many people consider such moments to be very spiritual. In my experience as a teacher of martial arts and as a personal empowerment consultant, I've had lots of discussions with people about the connection between the mind and the heart, or as I said in Chapter Three, the mind of the heart and the heart of the mind.

> One man I knew, his name was Al, was a hard-living man; a successful entrepreneur; and also a tough-looking, hard-talking biker—a member of a recreational motorcycle club. He was never in any real trouble with the biking life but he did know how to look after himself.
>
> One day he came into my office and I could see by his expression that something had changed for him. There was a softness in his features that wasn't there before. He said that he had just become a father, that his wife had just had their first baby. He described lifting the baby up to his large chest and looking for the first time into his daughter's newborn eyes, and he fell utterly and completely in love. He felt a depth of emotion he had never felt before.
>
> All of a sudden we were not talking about mind stuff or about conflict resolution or about how to be the warrior in our own lives. We were talking about love. The heart opening he experienced enabled him to become a caring and involved father. But, more important, it caused him to change how he interacted with the world. He was a warrior type. He didn't like to negotiate things. He just took what he wanted through force of will. Now, he is more conciliatory—a warrior still, but

with the capacity to be aware of hidden dynamics, unseen emotions. His awareness expanded. His life took on a new flow of energy.

How did he do that? He did it by gazing into the eyes of a newborn child and he knew with the clearest awareness he had ever experienced that a fixed and rigid attitude has no place in life, that life is an interplay of energies, and that there is inner safety in resting in the heart of the mind where "hassles" do not cause anxiety and where frustrations do not cause anger. His newborn daughter hit him with the whirlwind of love—and changed him forever.

Reminders to Your Warrior Mind

1. When we use the phrase "daily life," we tend to mean the times when our life feels ordinary, when everything moves along more or less the way we expect it to. Some people see daily life as everything that happens between the milestones of our lives. Others see daily life as meaning Monday to Friday and not including weekends (or days off if your work schedule involves weekends).

2. We are creatures of habit. Very often, our concept of daily life is a defense against the feelings of anxiety and the hassles that disrupt our lives. We don't want to admit to ourselves that sometimes life just won't cooperate with our best-laid plans. We want to pretend we are always in control.

3. By relegating most of our life to the realm of "daily life" and not paying attention to it, we rob ourselves of the im-

mediacy of the moment. Lulling ourselves to sleep through the routines of daily life can prevent us from savoring the unexpected treasures we may encounter in a day. It can also prevent us from dealing appropriately with an unexpected hassle. You're much more likely to be blindsided when you're asleep at the switch.

4. Attentive curiosity is a daily energy. Try looking at everything in your day with a playful curiosity. The calmness of your mind will alert your instincts toward both pleasant surprises and unpleasant hassles, so that you can deal with them without anxiety.

5. What is the common denominator between each day and yourself? You. You are the common denominator of all your experiences. And so you need to take care of yourself during daily life so that you'll have the energies to meet the challenges of extraordinary times.

6. There are three areas you need to pay attention to if you're going to maximize the use of the six energies in your daily life. First, get enough exercise. Your body was made to move. Exercise elevates mood and energy. Second, eat healthy foods. And eat regularly. Third, get enough sleep. Chronic sleep deprivation can deplete all your energies. Make it your clear intent to balance exercise, nutrition, and sleep, so that the six energies will function well for you and keep you in optimum form.

CHAPTER 5

Handling Work Challenges

Nothing tests our mettle and ability to cope more than the big challenges of life: losing a job, going through a divorce, grieving the death of a loved one, being injured in an accident. The word "crisis" means "a situation of extreme danger or difficulty," but it also means "a turning point." So even good things that happen to us can pose a challenge to us, whether [...] meeting the love of our lives, getting [...] big promotion.

[...] in a crisis feel they don't have the [...] ility to come to grips with the situa-[...] ned. Both the mind and body go into [...] ng back into one of the six energies, [...] tick up and they wind up in conflict [...] others.

Being in crisis is a state of mind right next door to "fight or flight." Perhaps you've experienced that feeling of being frozen in place, where you don't know what to do or whether you're making the right choices. Think of all the people who right before their wedding become frozen with the last-minute thought, "Should I really go through with this? Am I making the right decision?" They react this way because getting married is a major turning point.

How can the six energies of the Shadow Warrior help with the big crises? In this chapter we're going to look at the big challenges that can affect our work lives and then in the next chapter we'll talk about relationships.

I know a young man, Bill, who got a job in New York City that he had bid for and won. It was his dream job, but the dream came to an end three months later when the parent company in England decided to close its North American offices. Now Bill had a crisis to deal with. He was suddenly unemployed, living in a very expensive city.

Bill was disappointed, of course, even disheartened for a period of time. But instead of spiraling into fear and helplessness, he considered his situation with attentive curiosity: *How ironic that I would lose a job so quickly that I worked so hard to get. I was just getting into the swing of things. I saw a long career ahead of me with this company. Now I know what my friends were going through after they lost their jobs. You feel a sense of loss, you feel anger, the awful taste of fear.*

He did not allow his disappointment to prevent him from taking a calm look at all the circumstances of the termination. . . . . He began to consider how he could use mental undulation to formulate an alternate plan.

Bill went into action. He sent an e-mail to the company's head office in England, letting it know that he would be sending a proposal. In that proposal, sent to the head office by courier, he pointed out that although the company no longer had an office in North America, it still had clients there. Might the company need someone to represent its interests with those clients?

The British company invited Bill to the head office to chat with the president and the vice president of international operations. Today Bill is a highly paid consultant with the company, with the mandate of looking after its North American interests.

Bill turned a crisis into an opportunity. He used calm attentiveness to survey his situation and think it through. He used mental undulation to come up with possible alternate paths. He validated his clear intent to work in the field he had chosen despite the setback. Then he grappled, or "took on," the challenge by sending the e-mail and letter. That set into motion the rolling wave he threw at the company (the suggestion that he could represent the company in North America), and its rolling wave back to him offering him a consultancy. Bill got what he wanted, and in time it proved to be even better than the initial job he loved so much.

So a crisis can lead you toward chaos or it can lead you toward peace.

In a crisis we often feel very vulnerable physically, psychologically, and emotionally because our security base has been threatened. A crisis, whether good or bad, can knock us off center and sometimes flat on our ass. The reflex action is to reject the threat and the feelings of fear and anxiety. Some people go into denial or try to find ways to distract themselves from their problems.

But resisting the feelings of fear just makes them grow stronger. It's far wiser to pull them to you instead. Accept the feelings, own them as yours, own the situation as your reality, and then move on to some mindfulness thinking to get yourself to a state of clarity and calmness.

Instead of, "Oh, God, what am I going to do?" you say to yourself, "Let me take a close look at exactly what's going on here" (*attentive curiosity*). Then you allow your mind to begin to show you possibilities for resolving the crisis (*undulation*). Just the very process of pulling back and evaluating will help calm your mind and emotions.

As your emotions are calmed, you will begin to feel safer. This is important, because without inner safety there will be no resolution. If you feel unsafe within yourself, you won't have the clarity to make good decisions to get yourself out of the crisis. The Shadow Warrior mind techniques will help you break the crisis–panicky emotions circuit.

Let's look at areas in our lives where we most often will encounter a crisis situation. The workplace is a good place to start—after all, that's where we spend a large percentage of our adult productive years.

The Workplace as a Psychological Battlefield

Despite all the hype we hear about ideal workplaces as being team oriented and collaborative, the fact of the matter is that workplaces, by their very nature, are competitive. A recent study revealed that almost half of employees across a wide variety of industries want to find another job or leave their career path altogether. The major reasons they gave for this were workload stress (too much to do in too little time) and interpersonal conflict (toxic bosses, annoying coworkers, harassment).

This doesn't mean that teamwork and collaboration don't work or that companies can't create a positive atmosphere. There are many examples of companies that do that for their employees, the kind of companies that win awards for "best places to work" or "best managed." If you work for such a company, you have struck gold. These companies know the truth of an expression I often use: "People go where they're wanted, stay where they're needed, and grow where they're cultivated."

But even if you work for the most enlightened company in the world, you're still going to have some battles. There is competitiveness even in the best companies. Why? Because workplaces are made up of people with certain skill sets, many of whom want to get ahead and be seen in a good light. Even if you have no aspirations for advancement, even if you are perfectly content in your current position, you still want to be seen in a good light.

This natural competitiveness turns things into a battlefield.

Consider the example of Mary, a sales rep in a heating and air-conditioning multinational. Mary's an assertive "can do" kind of individual with natural sales talent. Within six months she qualifies for the largest performance bonus, more than employees receive who have been there for over ten years.

> Mary's sales help the company meet its objectives and strengthen the place of the sales division within the company, thus protecting the other salespeople's jobs. But now Mary faces a big problem with her colleagues. You could cut the resentment with a knife. Who is this upstart to come in and show off like that?
>
> Mary shouldn't give up her desire for success or dull her ambitions. But she is going to have to be vigilant. She has to know that she is perceived as a threat and that she needs to frame her sales in a way that shows their benefit to the team as well as the company. She has to take care of herself within the business model of her company. But she certainly can't fool herself that her company is devoid of internal competition, conflict, and envy.

Even in nonprofit companies that serve a humanitarian good, people compete for status and to be seen in a positive light. The goings-on in some nonprofit boardrooms as they compete for a slice of the nonprofit grant pie with other nonprofits can make corporate boardrooms seem like peaceful havens!

Having been involved in the military and business, I can draw a clear analogy between the two. Surviving in both requires having battle plans, because both involve battles. When it's a military battle, people get wounded and blood gets drawn. When it's a workplace battle, lots of psychological blood gets drawn. In the military if your leadership says, "There's the enemy, go engage them," you do. Likewise, businesses treat their competitors as "enemies" against whom they wish to win a larger market share, larger product volumes, and larger successes. And within companies, the same thinking can prevail: Union and management can be "enemies," one department can be the "enemy" of another, and some employees are seen as being "in your camp" whereas others are outsiders.

A little aside about plans. Here is a sampling of a few of the plans and planning strategies that I have been involved with to date. By no means complete, these are the ones that came to mind when I stopped to consider them: market plan, impact plan, fallback plan, threshold plan, time frame plan, sneak and peek plan, financial plan, shortfall plan, surplus plan, outsource plan, insource plan, upside plan, downside plan, attack plan, insertion plan, extraction plan, marriage plan, merger plan, withdrawal plan, go faster plan, go slower plan, stop plan, attack plan, review plan, attack again plan, be safe plan, do not be safe plan, go to guy plan, boss is happy plan, boss is pissed plan, get out of Dodge plan, review again plan, timing plan, take a break plan, break contact plan, vacation plan, and last but not least, let's move on plan.

Let's look at how you can plan to handle some of the battles you face.

Avoiding Friendly Fire

I have been on job sites where there have been numerous workers in a similar discipline (for example, electricians), all working on the same project. Although these individuals were part of "teams," the anxiety they felt that they were going to be outperformed by another team or by members of their own team caused all sorts of problems—and casualties. It gets just plain nasty and confusing when management is not able to harness all this energy and point the teams in the right direction.

You've heard of friendly fire, when soldiers are wounded or killed mistakenly by their own military. It happens on the job, too, when people who are supposed to be working with each other spend most of their time undercutting each other. Obviously it would be much better if they were all working together toward the same departmental or company objective.

The challenge is to move from competition anxiety to creative energy.

What if you are in this type of situation? What should you do? My advice is that you stop worrying about what the other folks are doing or about where your "place" is. That just causes anxiety for yourself and everyone around you. You want to do what you do best. You want to focus on your own goal or target within that team, or individually. You won't get there by being anxious about what somebody else is doing or not doing. You're going to get there by asking questions of the right people as to what the goal is and linking that with your own command of your own expertise.

This is a process of having a clear picture in front of you. When you get the picture, you create a pathway for your participation in the picture. Combine the strategies of *attentive curiosity* and *clear intent*. Get straight on what your role is and get a picture of how your role combines with other people's roles.

This kind of mind-set doesn't apply just to people employed by businesses to fulfill a job or career mandate. It applies also to entrepreneurs who as business owners need to know how to get a clear picture of where they fit in the marketplace and of how to create the pathway that will most effectively help them navigate that marketplace.

One of the best strategies to use when you're caught up in workplace battles is to realize that all things are temporary and impermanent. The only constant in the universe is change. We often have our identities so tightly bound to our jobs and positions that we see ourselves as being in a permanent structure, and so when change happens—when someone outstrips our abilities, when there's a layoff, or we're given a change in job responsibilities—we react with anxiety.

The Shadow Warrior mind-set, however—of awake, aware, attentive—shows you that nothing is permanent. There is only so far you can go with any situation. You've no doubt heard the expression, "This too shall pass." It's a little gem of wisdom to keep in the back of your mind every day on the job. That doesn't mean that you don't feel the emotions or that you teach yourself not to care about anything. It just means that, as a personal discipline, you retain in the back of your mind the fact that permanence is an illusion. Knowing that, there is no reason to fear impermanence or to fear the anxieties or unpleasant events that might happen to us in our lives. You may not like the anxieties, but you won't fear them, if you know in your very being that "this too shall pass."

The fallback position in the face of anxiety is the energy of *attentive curiosity*. Your ability to look calmly at what is going on around you and inside you is a fundamental disciplinary skill for getting through life with a calm inner center. Even in the most emotional situations, it is possible to step back in your mind and ask yourself, "What is happening here? What am I seeing? What am I hearing? What am I feeling? What am I perceiving?"

It's this energy of being able to calmly observe and evaluate your direction and purpose in any situation that will lead you very naturally to the energy of *mental undulation:* the entertaining of new possibilities and ideas, an undulation around whether you want to stay and work with the energies in the situation or whether you want to go in a different direction and leave the situation behind.

Undulation will lead you to your own innate creativity and resiliency. At that point, it starts to matter a lot less how competitive you are with someone else. You take responsibility for the only thing in life for which you have absolute responsibility: yourself.

Let's look at some workplace areas where we most often feel that we're in a battlefield and where fear and anxiety can interfere with our ability to function effectively.

The Job Interview

When I talk about using the six energies in a job interview, I'm not talking about pointers that will help you get a job. There are plenty of books out there on how to write a dynamite résumé, how to dress, and how to present yourself. What I'm talking about is the ability to get through a job interview and feel inwardly safe and confident throughout the process, whether or not you end up getting the job. That said, going through job interviews with such a calm and clear demeanor of collectedness and centeredness will increase your chances of getting the job. Calm self-confidence no doubt will impress your interviewers.

But you also need to know that self-confidence and qualifications alone will not automatically clinch a job. There are so many other factors—intangible factors such as the personality match between interviewer and interviewee, the match between your qualities and the workplace culture of the organization. There is a great deal of subjectivity involved in a job interview. That's why I am a job interview contrarian. I go counter to the conventional advice people give job hunters to "believe you are going to get that job, see yourself as already having the position." That kind of positive attitude *might* increase your chances. But *my* contention is that when you go for a job interview, you really don't know whether you want that job at that company because you have not yet been exposed to the culture of that workplace and the personalities in it. You can't possibly know that until after the interview.

CLEAR INTENT

So now maybe you're asking, "What about *clear intent?* Shouldn't I have a very clear intent about getting the job?" The answer is yes; however, make sure that the intent is not directed toward the company you've applied to, but rather to the type of position itself—a job that quite likely exists at numerous other companies as well. In other words, focus your clear intent on the macropicture of the type of position you're seeking, and not on the micropicture of individual companies you happen to interview with.

ATTENTIVE CURIOSITY

With the Shadow Warrior mind-set you will not think of a job interview as a pitch for a job. You will think of it as an experience you are going to have. You're going to have the experience of doing a job interview. You're going to go through it with a mental posture of *attentive curiosity*. It's an experience, nothing more—an experience where you will learn more about yourself and more about others who are hiring people in your field. It might help you to think of yourself as a newspaper reporter. Think of yourself as doing a story on company X and whom the company wants to hire. Go in there with a list of questions in mind. Look around. See what's going on. Get information, observe, assess.

How do you have a positive and calm experience in a job interview? Go into it with no expectations. Go into it with a mind-set of wanting to discover what is there. Do not try to get the job. Have no expectations about it whatsoever. Don't get trapped in the mentality of expectation. Remember that in Chapter 3 I talked about how your mind can be a great trickster. One of its favorite tricks is expectations. If you can let go of expectations, you let go of fear. Just experience the process. Of course you are going to do your best to present yourself in the very best light and it is crucial that you do so, but do it because that is who you are and what you have to offer.

Your clear intent is to present yourself in the best light possible, to highlight your skills and experience, to communicate why you are seeking a position in that particular field, and to *find* a job in that particular field. It's not about finding a job with that company; it's about finding a job where you can use your skills and talents to the max. It may be with that company but it may not be. Don't de-energize your clear intent with feelings like, "Oh, God, I really have to get a job with this company and if I don't, I'm a failure." No, you don't have to get a job with that company; what you have to do is get a job that reflects your talents and abilities, to find the right environment where your work will be valued.

There is a Buddhist saying: "If you are facing in the right direction, all you have to do is keep walking." This means that if your intent is clear about what you want, you'll get there. If it's not with that particular company, it will be with another company. If that door doesn't open, another will.

Everyone wants a really good job—a job where you're challenged, you're fulfilled, you're rewarded, you're not jumped on if you make a mistake, a job where you can experience professional and personal growth. Let that be your clear intent. There is a difference between clear intent and expectations. You can have a clear intent *and* have no expectations. That may seem paradoxical, but it isn't. What it means is that you know the parameters of what you want but you do not impose expectations onto specific circumstances.

If you don't impose expectations onto your job interview, you can enter into the experience of it. Your mind can be in a place of calm observation. You can ask yourself, "I wonder what this experience will be like?" In the back of your mind, you will be continually observing, even as you are engaging in conversation. You're just letting it all unfold.

Know this: Your sense of presence is far more important than all the techniques you may have learned about self-presentation in an interview. By all means, employ all the techniques you know about how to dress, when to shake hands, being respectful, showing enthusiasm, and so forth, but realize that it is your sense of presence, of "being there" in your own body without expectations about the result, that will convey a very impressive sense of calm collectedness to your interviewers.

MENTAL UNDULATION

If you're in this calm mind state, your mind will be able to engage in the *mental undulation* necessary for the job interview. It's very common in job interviews to be asked questions that require you to engage in mental undulation. By keeping your mind in observer status (attentive curiosity), you'll be prepared.

Imagine yourself being interviewed as one of several candidates for a middle-management position. During your interview, you're given the following scenario in which both your time management skills and your decision-making prowess will be tested:

> *Typically, your reporting, scheduling, and people demands significantly compress your time availability so that any additional demands on your time would cause you some significant challenges with the completion of your daily tasks. As can happen, you receive an immediate request from your divisional manager for a report summary that is needed now and not next week, as originally planned.* How would you handle this situation?

You might freeze up when faced with a hypothetical situation like this. A lot of people do. This challenge to your thinking is caused by the surprise element. You hadn't expected to be asked to play this little game. There seems to be no way to organize it. You are on the spot. If you're like a lot of people, you'll start blathering.

You might respond by thinking, "Oooooh, man, just when I thought I was on top of everything, a new challenge is thrown at me that I don't have time for." Well, you can spend your time with a nice bout of "stinkin' thinkin'" or you can connect with the six energies and use one or more of them as applied tools to bring about the resolution of your daily challenges. This is where breaking things down into the six energies can be very helpful. Just walk the situation through with your interviewer, step by step. The solution will come to you as you go.

- *Attentive Curiosity:* Portray yourself as taking a step back and regarding this new challenge with the open-mindedness needed to resolve this type of scheduling conflict, as opposed to reacting in anger, resenting how other people's problems are being dumped on you. Remember, you had planned this day with not a minute of spare time and now a directive from your superior is threatening to derail your carefully laid plans.

- *Mental Undulation:* Show how in moving from an attentive curiosity toward a mental undulation you're going to be looking at alternatives for the most appropriate way in which to handle this assignment, including checking first to see if the boss remembers that the summary wasn't supposed to be due for another week, looking over your schedule to see if a meeting today can be batched with a meeting that's planned for the next day, and so on. You would consider whether you were the only one from your department who could attend certain meetings, and whether someone else could write the summary for your boss while doing it in a way that your day does not have to change significantly.

- *Clear Intent:* This is where you really get to the core reason for this exercise and will show the interviewer your understanding and skill and strength—by bringing out into the open what your desire is: to take care of your boss's problem but not at the expense of your own plans and the overall good of your department. By no means is there only one way to bring resolution to this challenge, but for our purposes, we are going to suggest that you demonstrate clear intent by deciding to delegate this task to one of your senior assistant managers, who can then be given the guidelines and time frame needed to complete this task in the appropriate manner.

- *Grappling:* Let's say you tell the interviewer you have decided to call in your assistant and to give him the task of writing the report. Describe how you will get the key issues across to your assistant, asking for a draft on the main points that you can polish after your meetings. In this case, grappling with the relevant issues of making the report available to your superior would involve a meeting with your assistant in order to come to terms with the required dynamics that will make up the report.

- *Rolling Waves:* Portray yourself as rejecting and accepting the components of information that need to go into the report. To do this requires the attributes of rolling waves as a way to determine the necessary contents of the report by both discussing and rejecting and discussing and accepting which components of information need to be used to make up the report.

- *The Whirlwind:* This move is not necessary in this situation, but you could describe the kind of energy that's going to be called upon, on both your and your department's part, to solve the issue. The whirlwind is not necessary to use here in any other fashion than to be aware that time is of the essence.

When you have a grid like this—the six energies—you have something you can apply to situations, whether imaginary or real. In fact, you would do well to make up your own hypotheticals and imagine yourself handling them. This will help you work much smarter and with much greater focus.

Another aspect of mental undulation in an interview is for you to ask your own questions. Most interviewers ask the candidate whether she has any questions and very often the interviewee is tongue-tied, unable to think of anything to ask. But if you enter that room in a mind state of attentive curiosity and you listen to everything the interviewers say while in that mind state, plenty of questions will occur to you. (So make notes as you need to.) Make use of those questions. Ask the questions. The questions are a result of your mental undulations. If you can gain some control of the questioning process, you will be playing a role in guiding the interview. You won't be passive; you'll be active.

GRAPPLING

How does the strategy of *grappling* fit into a job interview? It comes into play when the interviewer describes to you how the company expects the job to be fulfilled. Grappling is taking on an issue, pulling it to you. So you begin this process of considering whether what he is describing to you is a match with what you want to do. At the grappling phase, your questions and answers become more specific, more focused. If something the interviewer says is unclear, ask for clarification.

Much of your grappling while this is going on is inner grappling. In your mind throughout the process you are wrestling inwardly with whether what is being presented to you fits what you want. You are considering whether you can live with those elements that do not fit what you want.

Let's face it, there's never going to be a perfect job. And so you're going to need to grapple with those parts of the job that may not be to your liking and you'll grapple also with the decision as to whether those parts of the job or the company would prevent you from wanting to be there at all.

Sometimes it can be the right job in terms of your preferences but the wrong company in terms of working conditions. Or it can be the wrong job but the right company. These are things you need to grapple with.

Often you will have lots of time for grappling—after the interview, while you're waiting for a response. If you felt that the interview went well, you can engage the grappling part of your mind when you get home to consider how you will answer if you get a callback that offers you the job. If you felt it didn't go well, or if you don't get a callback, the grappling process will help you discern what it is you really want in a job and in a company you want to work for.

ROLLING WAVES

The strategy of *rolling waves* will come into play if you do hear from the company. If you are called back for a second interview, it usually means you're on the short list of candidates or, even better, that the employer is prepared to offer you the position. Either way, the employer is going to get more into the nitty-gritty of the actual working parameters and conditions.

For example, the employer may throw this kind of wave at you: "This is the amount of vacation time, here is our sick leave policy, here's how our benefit plan works." Your response is to throw your own wave to them. If you are in complete agreement with everything she's offering, then your wave will indicate that. But if there are some details you'd like to negotiate further, you do it using rolling waves. If the employer says that vacation time is three weeks consecutive, you could throw a wave by saying that you would prefer two weeks consecutive and one week at a different time of year. Depending on the employer's response to that, you can negotiate further.

Remember that the idea of rolling waves is to roll in there with your comments, suggestions, and requests, and then to pull back and await the response. If you can get into this back-and-forth energy, it will keep you calm and centered. Very often, the most fearful part of job interviews is not the initial interview but the point at which the employer actually makes an offer. The reason for that is that now you know it's serious. If you accept, you will be committing yourself to that company and those terms of employment. So if you have any uncertainties, this is where they will come to haunt you and cause you anxiety.

Use rolling waves to alleviate this anxiety. They can help you get a clear picture of how flexible your employer is and what you are most comfortable with. The energy of rolling waves will clarify points for both you and the employer.

If after all this you are offered the job and you say yes, you will be coming to that job with absolute clarity of intent and

feeling good about how the energies played out in the interview. In a sense you will have already begun to integrate yourself with that company's culture.

If you don't get the job, don't sweat it. You have lived
through the experience, you have learned many things, and
you move on to the next interview. The important thing is
that you went through the experience from a place of inner
calm, not fear. You went through it without expectations. You
have presented yourself as an in-control person who is not
afraid to engage in a constructive discussion.

THE WHIRLWIND

You are not likely to use the energy of *the whirlwind,* our
sixth energy move, in a job interview. There are certain types
of industries, however, where pulling out all the stops in how
you present yourself may be valuable. Examples would be the
media, advertising, entertainment: careers where flamboy-
ance, boldness, and creativity are valued. In that kind of setting, you might choose to bombard your prospect from all
sides with a vibrant and bold presentation and a pumped-up
enthusiasm that surrounds your prospect with your energy.

Before opting for a super-high-energy demeanor, however, make sure you have researched the company's culture,
because the whirlwind, if it's used in the wrong place, could
damage your chances. Straightforward, forthcoming, and
businesslike with a modicum of enthusiasm is the order of the
day for most interviews.

~

Everything I have said about going through a job interview
applies equally to an entrepreneur looking at setting up his

own business. If you're an entrepreneur, it won't be job interviews you're going to, but rather meetings with potential clients, funders, suppliers, and so forth. You'll need exactly the same mind-set of attentive curiosity in order to determine your clients' needs and your financiers' requirements. You'll definitely need a lot of mental undulation to explore all possible ways you could structure your business and take it to the marketplace. You need a clear intent to know exactly what your business is and to make a dynamite business plan.

From there, rolling waves helps you in acquiring clients and in negotiating good deals with suppliers. The whirlwind can help you in how you market yourself, how you impact the market with great energy so that your company will get noticed.

All these processes require one-on-one interaction with people, just as a job interview does. And, the irony is that if you become a successful entrepreneur with your own business, it will be you who sits in the interviewer's chair interviewing prospective employees for your company. Think of how much more effectively you'll be able to structure and guide interviews when you're aware of the energies involved in the interview situation.

The Performance Evaluation

Performance appraisals are a part of business life. Most of us want to know how we're doing in a job, what our strengths are, and how to improve. However, the mere fact that the assessment is written down and creates a permanent record can cause anxiety. You know that the appraisal could follow you throughout your career. You also know that performance ap-

praisals sometimes get mixed up with the political environment of a company and the subjectivity of its own managers.

I heard of one company that appeared to deliberately assess
the majority of employees as "average" so that the company
wouldn't have to give out too many performance bonuses. In
another company, a manager admitted giving a competent employee a lower rating just so that the employee would get frustrated and eventually leave, all because the manager did not
like the employee's personality.

Another manager didn't like the idea of people getting mad
at him and so he tended to make the reviews overly positive.
Yet another reported that the process of evaluation made her
uncomfortable because of its tie to money. "Whenever a decision involves money, it can get emotional and uncomfortable
for both the manager and the employee," she said.

Like the job interview, a performance evaluation is a testing ground. You're being compared with a standard, having
your accomplishments compared with other employees or
candidates. And despite all the human resources literature out
there analyzing the components of a good performance appraisal and extolling the virtues of employee development, the
process of going through an evaluation still in many cases
feels like a one up, one down sort of transaction. By definition,
the evaluation is performed by a "higher" person on a "lower"
person. This type of power imbalance automatically causes
anxiety and makes you feel less safe.

Similar to a job interview, subjectivity enters the situation.
Perhaps your evaluator is in a bad mood that day. Maybe she
is someone with whom you don't get along. Maybe her view
of what constitutes "doing a good job" and your view differ.
Even when evaluation documents have extensive and seem-

ingly objective checklists of target goals and whether you reached them, there is still subjectivity.

You should acknowledge to yourself from the outset that these elements do play a role in evaluations. The question is how to get through the "crisis" of the mandatory annual or semiannual performance review without feeling anxiety.

The six energies can help here, too.

ATTENTIVE CURIOSITY

Your number one defense against feeling anxiety is to go into that room with an attitude of attentive curiosity—the first energy move. Just as in the job interview context we talked about earlier, don't let expectations, either positive or negative, color your awareness. Do not have any expectations of outcome. What you're dealing with is receiving facts and indicators and opinions about your performance. Your clear intent when you go in there is to uncover the truth of how you're doing, taking into account all the subjective factors that come into play.

The number one attitudinal tool is to not take anything personally. It is difficult to stay out of this mind trap during an evaluation. Our identities are so bound up with our job that we take any criticism as a reflection on us personally. The same is true if the evaluation is glowing. We allow ourselves to feel pumped up by a highly positive evaluation. It's good to rejoice in one's accomplishments, but don't make the mistake of identifying yourself—your Self—with any role or task. You are not your job. Your role or task is just one component of your life—not your entire life.

UNDULATION

The energy of undulation can help you when you've engaged in dialogue, and you've gauged where you're at in terms of your performance. You've now taken into account the subjective factors influencing the evaluator. If there are areas where you need to improve or new goals you need to set, engage the evaluator in considering ways you could accomplish that. The Shadow Warrior uses the energy of the opponent to his own advantage, yet without harming the opponent.

In this kind of situation, you take the energy roused by the evaluator's identification of your improvement areas and you initiate the brainstorming process to come up with a solution rather than waiting for the evaluator to do it. You take control of your own improvement and lead the evaluator toward your goals. This is a very empowering position to be in, and it will likely result in a win-win for both you and the evaluator.

GRAPPLING

Just sitting and listening passively to an evaluation and then signing on the dotted line only increases anxiety. It's better to use the energy of grappling. Take on each point raised in your evaluation. Pull it to you. Look at it. If you disagree with the evaluator, say so and state why. Engaging with your evaluator, asking questions, seeking clarification, expressing your own viewpoint—these things will help make you feel centered and alive and will lessen the anxiety.

When the evaluation zooms in on areas of weaknesses or where you need to improve, go to that space in your mind where you don't take anything personally. This is hard to do, because criticism almost automatically arouses defensiveness. A famous stage actor once said, "There is no such thing as constructive criticism; it's still criticism." By knowing ahead of time that it's perfectly natural for you not to like "constructive criticism," you can hold that in your awareness and prevent it from derailing you into trash talking yourself inwardly while you're listening to the evaluator.

See the evaluation as talking about your external performance, not about the inner you. Then, by grappling with these findings, you can arrive at a calmer assessment of whether or not you agree.

ROLLING WAVES

Going into the rolling wave energy can take you into dialogue. When your evaluator says something that you feel needs clarification or you need to provide further information to explain yourself better, roll in there with that "wave" and then wait for the response. When the evaluator's wave comes back to you, don't immediately jump into another point. Pause and consider. It's okay to have thoughtful pauses. If brief periods of silence bother you, simply say, "Give me a minute to think about that."

Workplace Conflict and Intimidation

What about when a situation at work becomes toxic, when you have to deal with a difficult coworker or boss, when the morale of the company is negative? I'm not going to go into all the steps you can take in specific situations. Each company will have policies and procedures, either formal or informal, for dealing with conflict situations. Instead, I'm going to focus on what keeps you inwardly safe, how you can keep your bearings, and some broad-stroke approaches you can use.

As I've mentioned, Shadow Warriors know how to use the energy to their own advantage. By going into your "awake, aware, attentive" mind state, you extend your mind to be able to embrace everything that's going on around you. Your mind is reaching out beyond your own anxiety to take a look at what's going on. You're getting beyond yourself in order to protect yourself.

When you have *attentive curiosity*, you stand without judging. You're simply seeing what's there. The "warrior of merit," to use a phrase from the martial arts, has self-respect and extends that respect to others. When the warrior's self-respect is attacked, he responds from a place of *clear intent* to maintain that respect. That means not jumping to conclusions, but staying in the mode of attentive curiosity so that your emotions will not be triggered and put you in a weak position.

Let's use the example of someone using derogatory language toward you or your colleagues. Your attentive awareness takes in the words without reacting to them. Then you use *mental undulation* in the form of calmly inquiring, "Did you mean to say that?" or "Did I hear you correctly?" Often, asking an intimidator to repeat the insult is enough to embarrass her into backing off.

After you've used the undulation energy to "move around" the insult, move to your *clear intent.* Your intent here is that the derogatory language is not going to stand. You make it clear to the person in a calm way that you feel the derogatory terms are not appropriate and you give that person a chance to retract without losing face.

Intimidators often respond with, "Oh, I'm just kidding" or

"Oh, you're just too sensitive." Now you have to go to the *grappling* position, by pointing out to the person that you are serious about not liking the way he is speaking to you, and asking him why he felt the need to address you in that way. Very often, that will be enough to make him back down and think twice before using words like that around you again.

If that doesn't work, you throw your *rolling wave*. You ask if the person would like to discuss the disagreement regarding the insult with a third party, such as your supervisor. You wait for the response. If you're not happy with the response, you can then unleash *the whirlwind* by making a formal complaint yourself to your superiors, outlining, both verbally and in writing, everything you did to attempt to resolve the situation.

The warrior of merit stays calm, simply taking in the situation. The Shadow Warrior sees the unseen. What is unseen about a harasser or intimidator? That he is not coming from a place of power, but of fear. The Shadow Warrior knows that the person carries a lot of fear inside. The only way the person feels he can look better in other people's eyes is to continually criticize, harass, or bully others verbally. The only way that person feels safe is to invalidate others.

The Dalai Lama says that we should show compassion toward anyone behaving negatively because such a person is unskillfully trying to alleviate his own inner suffering. This doesn't mean that you condone what the person is doing or that you get all warm and fuzzy toward him. It simply means that you can keep a clarity of mind in knowing that he is trying to alleviate his own inner suffering, and when you realize that, you learn the great wisdom of not taking things personally. Not taking things personally frees you up to be creative in how you deal with the conflict.

What does the skilled warrior do in observing an intimidator, an invalidator? Observe the structure of the person who is trying to intimidate and look for the cause. By "structure," I mean the person's characteristic way of communicating. If the person is nice to everyone else but is trying to intimidate *you*, there is going to be a different cause from the person trying to intimidate everyone.

If the person slumps and appears downcast in unguarded moments, this could tell you that the person is using aggression to hide depression. If the person becomes intimidating only when his own boss is around, this could tell you that he is trying to gain favor with his boss at your expense. An intimidator has to make you look bad in order for him to feel that he is somehow superior to you. As wrong as this may be, it is practiced frequently.

Above all, you experience your greatest power in yourself when you realize that you don't even have to respond emotionally. You don't have to react to the intimidation. You can create a psychological shield around yourself, a shield that is made up of your own keen awareness and the knowledge that you don't have to take things personally. You can practice mental undulation and grappling from a clear place inside of yourself to help you decide what to do about the situation.

If you have considerable spiritual strength and mental clarity, someone's attempts to wound you will have no impact. What's more, that person is going to intuit that his bullying is not making an impression. Bullies don't seek out awake, aware people. They seek out insecure people who react to external cues. You can make an inner decision to refuse to be intimidated. Nobody can create a reality for you that you do not assent to. Knowing that deep in your bones keeps you inwardly safe. You are the person who decides which influences to let in and which to keep out.

I once witnessed a judoka match between a Korean black belt and a Russian black belt. The Korean was huge: six feet, seven inches, and almost 300 pounds. The Russian was five feet, ten inches, and 200 pounds. You'd think the Korean would have won the match, but not so. The Russian could see that the Korean was attempting to intimidate him by his size, but he knew that a taller and heavier fighter is going to have a worse fall because of the forces of gravity. The Russian took advantage of that and it was over in the blink of an eye. He had refused to be intimidated by what the Korean was project- ing. And I'm sure that the Korean picked up on those cues— "Uh-oh, this isn't working." He was projecting false confidence, and so it didn't take much to cause him to have no confidence.

If your opponent is using intimidation as a tactic, it's be- cause she feels that you have something she doesn't have. If an intimidator confronts you, you are the one with the power, no matter how scary or offensive the intimidator is.

If you are being harassed or intimidated at work, follow whatever procedures your company has in place to deal with that. Do it from a place of inner calmness and observation, not from a place of fear. Keep your emotions in these circum- stances under the tight control of emotional knowledge. If the resolution is unsatisfactory, you keep at it until you get the result you want (rolling waves or the whirlwind).

The warrior of merit also knows when a battle is not worth fighting. If your workplace is so toxic that it begins to affect your health and your emotional morale, you may choose to just get out. There are other workplaces. You do not have to subject yourself to continuing toxic conditions. The impor- tant thing is that *you* decide what your path will be—after carefully observing and measuring the situation (attentive cu- riosity), considering alternatives (undulation), deciding that you are not going to be intimidated or harassed (clear intent), taking on the situation by addressing the details (grappling), attempting resolution by making your case known and awaiting a response and continuing that process until resolution (rolling waves), and, if necessary pulling out all the stops by going to the top of the company or the press (the whirlwind).

At any point in the process, you can undulate to another possibility, including the possibility of just walking away. Use your fallback position of attentive curiosity to help you discern what your decisions should be at every step.

Handling Serious Setbacks: Losing a Deal, Layoffs, Getting Fired

If you're an entrepreneur and you lose one of your major clients, you've taken a hit. If you're an employee or an executive of a downsizing company and you get laid off, you've taken a hit. If you get fired, you've taken a hit. These days it's almost impossible to be in the world of work and not have experienced one or more of these events.

It's very natural that your reaction is going to be one of fear and anxiety. When the economic basis of our lives is threatened, there is fear. The questions, "What am I going to do?" and "How am I going to live?" race through your head. It doesn't matter when you read that most entrepreneurs at some point in their careers experience business losses, or that most people at least once in their lifetime will be laid off or fired. When it happens to you, you experience it as a crisis.

A spiritual warrior mind-set such as I have been describing in this book does not mean rejecting the very real emotions and fears that arise in situations like this. If indeed you have come to practice the discipline of attentive curiosity, awakeness, and awareness in your life, you are in a position to allow the feelings without the feelings overwhelming you.

> I watched a friend of mine, Stan, a contractor dealing with a significant investment in new equipment, go through a setback where his cash flow all but dried up. He had been through this before in his career but when it happened yet again, he said to me, "I will never get used to being fired by my clients. I hate it with a passion. It doesn't matter what the reason is; it doesn't matter that it's all about market forces and it happens to everyone, and so forth. It still hits you right between the eyes."
>
> Instead of saying, "I'm not going to feel that way," he said, essentially, "I feel that way and I'm jumping up and down about it. If I feel like cussing, I'm going to cuss. If I have to go off by myself for a while, that's what I'm going to do." Stan understood that in the face of a major job setback, he was going to feel bad. He didn't waste his warrior's energy on trying not to feel bad.
>
> Once Stan felt satisfied that his personality was still intact, his mind went to an attentive curiosity. He said, "Okay, as a curiosity I wonder what my path is through this? I'm going to use some creative thinking on myself (undulation) and I'm going back to the basics of beginner's mind and I'll stay there until my pathway opens up."
>
> That's exactly what he did. Stan decided that he had to review his standard operating procedures in the belief that he would discover the keys necessary to improving his company's offerings to its clients. He also

believed that its investment in new equipment and process support equipment should allow him to bid on larger jobs. In a summary to himself, Stan implemented a review process that included policies, procedures, staffing, and material requirements.

He had a very highly skilled workforce who really enjoyed the working environment. His employee turnover was due more to retirement and moving than to workplace dissatisfaction and morale problems. His people were the backbone and strongest asset he had to offer to his clients. One of the major contributing reasons for this was his belief in upgrading his people. He believed that if they were given numerous opportunities to go through in-house and vendor-sponsored training programs, they would feel that the company cared about them; that the company cared about their involvement in where the company was going and their contribution to that process.

He knew that his company was certainly ahead of his competitors in terms of both quality and scope of his mission statement. He could now focus on creating an aggressive and forward-looking marketing program.

Before doing this, however, he wanted to summarize the contributing factors to making his marketing plan based on a thorough knowledge of what his company could do that his competitors could not do. He focused on the following factors:

1. His competitors' equipment was on average twelve years older than his.

2. His competitors' administration system was based on handwritten work orders and invoices.

3. Their inventory, receivables, and payables tracking were being managed by manual ledger tracking.

4. Only 11 percent of the staff at his competitors' companies had been with those companies for five years or more, compared with 45 percent of Stan's staff having been there over five years.

5. The average salary of workers at his competitors' companies was about four dollars per hour less. This was one of the prime reasons that they could undercut Stan's job site quotes. His competitors paid no performance bonuses to anyone under supervisor level, and when those supervisors were paid, it was based more on political than performance considerations.

After reviewing and summarizing, Stan decided to offer his past, current, and potential clients guarantees of performance completions with early bonus considerations. In addition, Stan offered these same clients a no fault clause if the job had time overruns due to his people and not the clients.

It wasn't long before the results became obvious. Stan's company didn't get really big in terms of dollar volume, but his company did get really healthy financially. It did add staff, and today his company enjoys a prosperity that comes from achieving a critical mass in terms of market acceptance of what his company does. Stan smiles a lot now.

The process takes time and you need to allow it to happen. You need to know that your emotions and even your mind will try to trick you into thinking this is the worst disaster that could ever befall you. If you allow the emotions and thoughts into your awareness, they can no longer trick you and you'll see that there is another side, a clarity and a calmness, from which you can evaluate your situation.

When martial artists get hit, they don't call it a setback. They call it an event. It's an event that causes pain, but it's viewed with a mind-set that all of life is change. It's viewed with the mind-set, "This is the circumstance and I have to decide what its impact will be on me."

You can take hits, too. When you look at your life as a series of events and experiences and you do not allow your emotions to back you into a corner, you will be able to recover enough presence of mind within yourself to know that there is always something you can do, always a pathway that allows you to get back up after the hit. Perhaps it's to change your type of business or reframe how you do business. Perhaps it's to return to school for further training. Perhaps it's to make a career change. Perhaps it's to relocate geographically. Perhaps it's to retire early. Your mind can show you many scenarios when you allow it to undulate past the fear and anxiety.

> John, a friend of mine who worked for a pest control company, was doing very well in his job, so well that the company offered him a franchise. A few months later, the parent company foundered and pulled the plug. John found himself without a franchise, without the $35,000 he had invested in it, and without a place to go to work the next morning.
>
> John is also a skilled kickboxer, which is why he

summed up his feelings this way: "This feels like a really bad body shot." He hadn't seen it coming. But because of the inner wisdom he had gained from learning fighting techniques, he acknowledged that the hit had come and gave himself time to understand what had happened.

He went through a mental undulation process for about two months. He talked to a lot of people and let it be known what his skills were and his own entrepreneurial abilities. Then he got a call from the competitors of his former company, asking him if he would consider working for them and that they would guarantee his income for a year initially.

We had a beer together shortly after this and he couldn't stop smiling as he described how he had been taken off his feet but had gotten up again.

Remember that the most effective place from which to fight a battle often is from down on the mat. Paradoxically, the times when we're at our lowest is where we find the strengths in ourselves that will show us another way. When you can disengage your identity from your job, you come to understand that you are so much more than your job, and that life can deal some hard blows but that you are more than enough to deal with them.

Reminders to Your Warrior Mind

1. Being in crisis is a state of mind right next door to fight or flight. The word "crisis" means "a situation of extreme danger or difficulty," but it also means "a turning point." The

Shadow Warrior knows how to use crises as turning points, which then become opportunities for growth and progress in his life path.

2. The workplace is a psychological battlefield in many respects. No matter how good workplaces are in terms of encouraging teamwork and rewarding people with recognition for a job well done, it's still the case that our workplaces are competitive environments. Workplaces are made up of people with skills and abilities, many of whom want to get ahead and be seen in a good light.

3. Take a bit of a contrarian view toward job interviews. Much of the popular wisdom tells you to approach a job interview with the intent of getting that job. But it's a far more powerful stance to go into the interview without expectations and an attitude of exploration of possibilities. You can use each of the six energies in a job interview, and no matter what the outcome, you will have conducted yourself with a calm confidence.

4. Performance evaluations are a testing ground. Many people become defensive about performance evaluations. Your number one defense against feeling anxiety is to not take anything personally. You are not your job. The energies of undulation, grappling, and rolling waves serve you well during an evaluation by making you an active participant in taking control of your own improvement and career path.

5. In dealing with workplace intimidation or harassment, you experience the greatest power in yourself when you realize

that you do not have to respond emotionally. The six energies can act as a shield that gives you calmness and clarity. If you tap into the inner strength of the six energies, you will become the one who decides how to reach a place of resolution, not other people's agendas.

6. Job loss is "taking a hit." We may experience anger, grief, frustration, and a sense of losing our direction. When a martial artist takes a hit, he doesn't call it a setback. He calls it an experience. It's an event that causes pain but it's viewed with a mind-set that all of life involves change and that nothing is permanent. When you look at your life as a series of events and experiences and you do not allow your emotions or other people's power plays to back you into a corner, you will recover the presence of mind within yourself to know that there is always something you can do, always a way to get back up after the hit.

CHAPTER 6

Handling Relational Challenges

When it comes to dealing with relational challenges wisely, the starting point is always your relationship with yourself. If you don't have self-awareness and an appreciation of who you are as a human being, you'll find that your relationships are going to be fraught with frustrations. By understanding your own reactions and "hot buttons," you can better understand others. By knowing your most characteristic way of dealing with all your life's issues and challenges, you'll get a better picture of how your personal orientation mixes with the orientations of others. You'll know why you get along with certain types of people and not with others. You'll know why certain people drive you up the wall while you find others a delight.

The six energies can be excellent tools for helping you discover a lot about yourself. If you take a look at the presence of the six energies in your life as we have been describing them in this book, you may notice that one or two of them seem to come more naturally to you. In other words, you may find yourself relying on one or more of your favorite energies as your overall approach to life. This can represent both a strength and a drawback—a strength in the sense that your particular favorite energy is well honed in your personality and so you use it smoothly and without conscious thought; a drawback in the sense that sometimes your favorite energy is the wrong one for the situation. If you're grappling when you should be using mental undulation, you'll find that the situation doesn't resolve the way you'd like it to. If you're sitting there being attentively curious and another person is using the whirlwind because he is really excited or angry, the communication between the two of you will not work, to put it mildly.

Which Energy Are You?

Let's look at the way the six energies can shed light on which energy *you* are and the relationship you have with yourself.

THE ATTENTIVE CURIOSITY TYPE

Some people are really good at observing. They seem to notice everything going on around them. They see details that everyone else misses. One famous fictional character who embodies this quality is Sherlock Holmes. The great detective solved crimes and found the perpetrator through the sheer ability to notice things everyone else missed. Sherlock Holmes was really good at attentive curiosity—"elementary, my dear Watson."

Any of you military types or those of you interested in Sneak and Peak terminology, which is used during LRRPs

(Long-Range Recon Patrols) or FRPs (Force Recon Patrols), know that the people trained and chosen for such missions are experts at noticing small, seemingly unimportant details that might elude the notice of a cursory glance. How important are these skills? Important enough to be able to tell the difference between friend and foe by how shoelaces are tied. The technique of using the fingers to "feel" this detail while not revealing your presence has been much used in jungle environments during conflict around the world.

If you're more of an observer than a participant, if you're a detail person, if you love to analyze things, and you put of lot of emphasis on noticing your environment, you're strong in attentive curiosity. You're the kind of parent of whom your child says, "Nothing gets past Mom [or Dad]. I can never get away with this!" You're the kind of boss about whom employees say, "She never misses a thing!" You're the kind of entrepreneur to whom your clients say, "You always seem to know what the customers need," or "You're really good at understanding marketing trends; you're always ahead of the game."

If any of this describes you, then one of your stronger energies is that of an attentive curiosity. If so, you're lucky, because attentive curiosity is the bedrock of all the other energies. So in that sense it's a great strength. The drawback, if this is your only strategic energy, is that you'll find it difficult to get things done or to actually make a decision. You'll need to develop the other energies to help you accomplish your goals, to go on from observing things to doing things.

THE UNDULATION TYPE

Some people are really good at generating ideas. They see new ways of looking at things. They are able to pay attention to many things at once. Undulation energy is a huge part of creativity. Creative individuals are not stuck in only one perspective. They're not afraid to think outside of categories. Originality and imaginativeness drive their personalities and their goals.

There are also people who always seem to look on the bright side, individuals who know how to make lemonade out of lemons. These are the people who say, "Never say never" or "There's always another way" or "Have you thought of this approach?"

If most of these qualities describe you, your favorite energy is undulation. This is a tremendous strength. It brings out your creativity. It gives you energy. Undulation types are usually high-energy people who are exciting to be around. The undulation type will always find an original way to do something or will be the one who finds the way out of a morass.

There's a drawback to being predominantly an undulation type, however. If that energy is not balanced by the other five, you may, like with the attentive curiosity type, find it difficult to make up your mind. You may not be able to stick to your guns and follow through. You may find it a challenge to turn your ideas into reality. The attentive curiosity type is too busy noticing details and so fails to make a decision. The undulation type is too busy coming up with new ideas or possibilities and fails to arrive at a decision. Different energies, but similar result.

THE CLEAR INTENT TYPE

Some people thrive on being decisive. They always seem to know what they want and what to do. They're the kind of person of whom it's said, "She is stubborn as a mule" or "Once she has made up her mind, there's no stopping her." These individuals stay focused on goals and like to measure their progress. They are often good at giving orders and tend to take a "command" approach to life.

If decisiveness and action are your comfort zone, you're a clear intent type. As a strength, having clear intent means you know what you want, and then go after it. It means that not much can deter you once you've made up your mind. The drawback is that sometimes you're so focused on being decisive that it's difficult for you to change direction when you need to. Or you may make your decision based on too little information. You don't want to appear indecisive, so you might cut corners in gathering the information.

Clear intent types can benefit by developing their attentive curiosity. And often they need the energy of undulation to loosen them up a bit.

THE GRAPPLING TYPE

Here's an example of the downside of a grappling personality:

> Some years ago, I ran a division of a company that was international in scope and developed and marketed several lines of direct fastening systems and electromagnetic drills. I had several sales reps who reported to me and an office support staff for the administration of the territories. We were consistently above our quotas in sales and our receivables ran 94 percent under sixty days. You'd think that the smile on my face was painted on.
>
> I had one sales rep whose territory produced about

12 percent over his forecasted sales and gross profit. We had done the forecasting for his territory and had it approved by the head office. We didn't know at the time that a major petrochemical plant that we would be supplying had been approved for construction with a hurry-up order for completion. We were very excited about the potential revenues that would be generated by this new plant—except for one person, the salesperson with the 12 percent over-forecasted sales.

This salesman was a graduate of the University of "Let's Keep Everything the Same and Not Do Anything to Rock the Boat." Every time the subject of servicing the site was brought up for discussion, Bill (not his real name) would remind me that this was not part of his contract, or that he simply could not find the time to service this site and keep up with the demands of his existing clients.

Let's look at one of Bill's main character traits. We looked for and found people who loved being creative and who could problem solve with a minimum of supervision. This required strong leadership tendencies with the potential for leadership skills training. The candidates had to be able to handle themselves with confidence and express skilled and complete technical knowledge relevant to the job at hand. Bill had all of this and more. As he was promoted and encouraged to participate in corporate training programs, he started to express disinterest and became withdrawn. He started to show the signs of burnout. He began showing up ten minutes late at branch meetings. Every time we asked him to let us know in advance if he would be late, he ignored the request.

When management introduced various incentive packages to promote new products, Bill would say that they weren't generous enough, or that the corporate picture was being built on his back, or that his clients didn't like that sort of thing and he saw no reason to push it. If I said up, he said down. If I said go right, he would go left. If sales for the region were off, he'd say, "I told you it wouldn't work." If sales of a new launch were way ahead of forecast, Bill would cover that by saying, "Just lucky, for such an amateurish launch."

He had a strong personality, his clients thought he was great, his sales were good, his attitude was . . . dreadful. It got to the point where his peers started asking him to stay away from their meetings. That's the destructive side of being a grappler and out of balance. Bill eventually left us and went into the oil business. Eighteen months later, his business became insolvent. Life can be nasty at times, particularly when a person chooses to harden his attitude and decides to grapple and fight with each and every thing that crosses his path.

You know this type, the people we call "scrappers" or "fighters"—people who stand their ground and go head-to-head with a person or an issue. This kind of person is not afraid of debate and argument.

If you're a grappling type, you "get into" things. You roll up your sleeves and jump right in there. You don't let things stand in your way—and if they are in your way, you grapple with them.

As a strength, grappling keeps you close to the action. It's a quality that helps you embrace life and not back off from challenges. As a drawback, it can pull you into needless conflicts and battles, as happened with Bill. Like him, some people just seem to want to fight and argue about everything. So if you're a grappler, add some undulation into the mix. And work on developing attentive curiosity and clarity of intent so that you'll pick your battles more wisely.

THE ROLLING WAVES TYPE

One of my staff, John (not his real name), called me for a meeting and told me that during a routine call with a client, he was told that the vice president of construction wanted to update all of their fastening tools and standardize their tooling program with one supplier servicing all of their branches. This is the kind of opportunity that companies dream about and salespeople lose sleep over. The initial value of the deal was in the mid–six figures plus the ongoing consumption of products at each of their branches. One little problem raised its head that threatened to destabilize and threaten the entire deal. Deals this size just do not come without a few challenges to overcome.

Their largest branch had a manager whose golfing buddy worked for a competitor of ours and he was not going to approve our deal and cut his buddy out of his supply chain . . . period. We went to the VP who initiated this and he confirmed that he wanted us in all of the branches. It had to be with the support of each of the branch managers. We spoke several times with the branch manager who was objecting, and we even complimented him for his support of his preferred supplier. We rolled waves at him in the form of various suggestions. He even agreed with the benefits to his company but didn't want to have to live with firing a good supplier who had become a good friend. He did have a point that we had to respect. We stayed with it for several months, hoping an opportunity would present itself that would allow us a pathway that would bring this deal to a conclusion in our favor.

I received a call from the dissident manager, who asked for a meeting and said that the other supplier's rep would like to attend. I agreed, and the next day I sat with the two of them. The other rep thanked me for not attacking his performance or his character. Instead, I had been very candid with my observations and evaluation of his performance to the manager without being patronizing. The rep then told me that his company was going through a major downsizing and he just found out that he was being replaced by someone half his age with 10 percent of his knowledge base. Would I be interested in recommending him for employment with my company?

I was truly speechless. I had spent a lot of time and energy trying to get these two people to my way of thinking. They knew this deal was important to my company and to me personally. The waves I kept throwing at them were clarity of intent and rolling waves that denoted a desire to do our very best for them as individuals and for their company as good corporate citizens. And how could I have guessed the wave they threw back? I ended up with the rep

the dissident branch manager had wanted to protect,
and the problem was solved!

A rolling waves person is not passive. She engages in action
but then withdraws to see what happens. The rolling waves
type says, "Okay, we've given it our best shot; now let's wait
to see what he says or does." She understands the rhythm of
taking action and then waiting.

A rolling waves person also has determination, but it's a
different kind from that of the clear intent type. Whereas the
clear intent type (without the moderating influence of the
other energies) will just keep plowing forward, the rolling
waves person figures out that sometimes the best way to realize her intent is through a strategic withdrawal.

As a strength, the energy of rolling waves gives you a sense
of timing and an inner barometer of how and when to expend
your energy. Rolling waves give you a marvelous combination
of persistence and flexibility. The drawback of rolling waves is
that it can be used manipulatively. You may withdraw from a
conflict just at the time when you should be grappling with it,
thereby leaving your opponent feeling that you're being un-
fair. Rolling waves types can benefit from having more grappling energy in their personality and also more undulation as
you come to understand the creative process of knowing
where and when to send your waves.

THE WHIRLWIND TYPE

This is a person we would call intense, volatile, stormy,
dramatic, passionate. Whirlwind types turn everything into a
dramatic scenario with larger-than-life characters and situa-

tions. They also unleash enormous energy in taking on challenges where they need to prevail. They're like a fast train coming down the tracks or a fast-approaching thunderstorm.

If you're a whirlwind type, you'll often raise the energy in the room and get everyone pumped. As a strength, the whirlwind energy makes you a force to contend with. It does make you formidable in battle. Motivational speakers are good at using the whirlwind energy to capture their audience's enthusiasm. There's a vitality in the whirlwind that can feel very empowering. Its drawback is that if you're not careful, you can knock over everything in your path. You can overwhelm people, coming across as an intimidator. Instead of being just colorfully dramatic, you can become a drama queen (or king)—a real pain in the ass. The whirlwind energy needs the input of all the other five energies in order to balance it.

~

In identifying which of the energies is your typical one, you may begin to see how they influence your pattern of relating to others. And you may also get a sense of why some relationship conflicts happen. Let's say you're an undulation type. You're always thinking up new things and attracted to new ideas. But you're married to a clear intent type who gets really frustrated that you just don't seem to make a decision, whether it's about what to have for dinner or what career to follow. You can just imagine the potential for conflict! If you're a grappling type involved with a whirlwind type, there are going to be a lot of fireworks in your relationship. If you're an attentive curiosity type involved with a rolling waves type, the rolling waves person may at times see you as a stick in the mud and the attentive curiosity person may spend more energy trying to analyze the rolling waves person than actually relating to her.

When you identify for yourself which one or two of these energies is dominant in your personality, that very self-awareness can free you up to begin consciously to develop the other energies. The more balance and flow you can achieve among the six, the more well rounded and balanced you will be. You will begin to realize the warrior mind and your relationships will be healthier and more rewarding as a result.

Feeling Safe in Relationships

Difficulties in our workplaces have the power to weigh heavily on our hearts, but difficulties in our relationships even more so. Human beings are wired for intimacy. We're pack animals. We need social groupings and pair bonding. Sometimes our desire for one-on-one intimacy conflicts with our desire for variety in relationships, leading evolutionary biologists, psychologists, and sociologists to wonder endlessly whether humankind is naturally monogamous or not. And the answer to that is likely both yes and no. (How's that for undulating around such a controversial question?)

Long-term relationships are challenging. My wife and I have often commented to each other that the most difficult thing we have ever done is stay in our relationship for more than thirty years. There's a huge challenge involved in having another person in your life whose life changes along with yours, and not always in the same direction. So it's a reality that for many people, when their partner's life begins going in a different direction, the relationship dissolves. Whether that different direction is a love affair, a move to a different career that may not be compatible with the existing family situation, personal growth into areas your partner has no interest in, or a spiritual change, the result can be an end to the relationship.

But certainly not always. There are indeed many good relationships of long standing all around us. In these relationships, a different direction can be accommodated and embraced without threat. Learning to master the six energies can help our relationships weather the natural ups and downs that occur in the lifetime of any meaningful intimate connection with another person.

Like everything else in life, marriage changes, friendships change. The paradox is that the more we try to keep everything the same, the more pressure builds up and you change. In fact, the only constant in life is change. The more you resist change, the more you hasten it and the more dramatic and unruly it will be in your life. Resist it and it will master you. Flow with it and you will master it.

So part of the Shadow Warrior mind-set on relationships is to accept that relationships change over time and that relationships go through cycles. This is as true of your colleagues at work and your friends as it is of your spouse or intimate partner.

> Picture this (and it's a true story): a large brewery employing upwards of 1,200 people. In particular we'll look at two people in the management echelon. One runs the infrastructure that keeps the beer flowing to the parlors, events, and hotels. The person he reports to has his respect and support in a way that makes the superior's job run smoothly. This relationship has run

this way for more than fifteen years. Senior management, for some reason, decides to make changes based on a consultant's report. The senior of the two individuals is promoted because of the excellence of his work and his reporting ethic. His junior is offered a package to leave and a package to stay. He chooses to stay, is demoted, and moves to a permanent night shift. Not very honorable, to say the least.

Perhaps at work you have a situation where you've always worked closely with a colleague, and the two of you have developed a strong friendship. Then you get promoted and your colleague does not, and you find that the dynamic has changed. If you resist the change and refuse to acknowledge it, you simply widen the gap between the two of you. By accepting that things have changed, you can look for ways around it in order to maintain the friendship. Or you may come to a point where you have to let it go. I think people cause themselves a lot of grief by hanging on to things and people when they should let go.

Of course when it comes to marriage or a live-in significant other relationship, we tend to have more invested emotionally there than with our work colleagues. We've made the commitment and we want to make it work. No one goes into a marriage or cohabitation situation expecting it to end. Yet when it does end, we learn to pick up the pieces and go on. The same for friendship—friendship is one of life's greatest joys and many of us will go through thick and thin for our friends and they for us.

In relationships, as in everything else in terms of the six energies, the fallback position needs to be attentive curiosity, an openness to see and understand what is there. It's so hard to do this in an intimate relationship. Intimate relationships are full of projections. We project onto the other person what we want him or her to be, our expectations, hopes, and dreams, and we're disappointed if the person doesn't live up to that. Or we react to our partner as if he were our father or as if she were our Aunt Mary who always annoyed us.

And what about children? If you're a parent, then you really know all about the changes a person and relationship can go through. Not just the changes of growing up from babyhood to adolescence, but also the changes within each of those stages.

A high school guidance counselor I know frequently gives talks to parents about the ups and downs of teenagehood. He always asks the question, "Do you ever feel that your kids are space aliens?" And the parents laugh knowingly. He then goes on to describe how he broke up a power struggle with his teenage son over dropping his clothes all over the floor. Let's let him tell it:

> You know you've got this space alien living with you, so you have to get the attention of the space alien. So how I did that with my space alien was to pick up his clothes off the floor and hang them all out on the tree on our lawn.
>
> "Daaaaadddd . . . what're you doing?" my son said, scowling and dragging all his clothes back into the house. But guess where he dragged them! To his closet!

We tend not to see our partners and our children as clearly as other people. We see those close to us through the filter of our own projections. The school guidance counselor's humorous tactic of seeing his teenager as a space alien is one way the father was able to withdraw projection from the son. The father didn't rail at the young man as a "messy person who has to be told over and over again to pick up after himself and who never listens" (a projection of his own standards of "not messy"). He made his point instead by throwing a rolling wave at his son (hanging the clothes in the tree). Both the father and his son came to see this as a joke, but the point was made, and the behavior changed.

The Shadow Warrior mind-set can help you set aside projection. Achieving a state of attentive curiosity about what's going on can keep you from being triggered into conflicts: hurt feelings, raised voices, psychological pushing and shoving. Your mind becomes trained to present something to you as a curiosity. That's much more calming and effective than kicking into an accusing or angry mode. Which is more effective? Going into a sulk, or saying to your partner, "You know what, I want to tell you how I'm feeling about what you just said [or did]"? The latter, of course,

If your ten-year-old daughter announces that she hates school, hates her teachers, and wants to leave and go live somewhere else, the attentively curious "Why are you feeling that way?" or "What's going on at school or here at home to make you feel that way?" is infinitely more effective than "Don't say such things about your teachers! And you have a perfectly good home here!"

Overly emotional reactions or reactions colored by projection tend to shut down communication. People turn off when they're the butt of someone else's negative emotions or projections. If your partner or child turns off, you don't have his attention. If you're going to be able to communicate clearly, you have to get the other person's attention and he has to get yours. Sure, sometimes strong emotion is an attention getter, and sometimes points have to be made emphatically. But more often than not, you'll find that the calming strategy of using attentive curiosity will work much more effectively in getting and keeping someone's attention and help both of you really communicate with each other.

You may find it helpful to look at your relationships as a day-to-day experience. Within that framework, the energy of mental undulation will serve you very well. So often in our relationships we grow more rigid rather than more flexible. We get accustomed to routines. But the path to vitality and satisfaction lies in flexibility—the ability to bend, the ability to sway, the ability to roll with it, the ability to see other points of view. Why do you have to vacation in the same location every year? Why does Thanksgiving always have to be at Uncle Joe's or Grandma's house? Maybe Uncle Joe and Grandma should come to your place this year. Maybe instead of camping at the seaside, you'll go hiking as a family in the Rocky Mountains.

Where does clear intent fit into relationships? If your relationship really matters to you, then you form a clear intent toward that relationship. You make a conscious commitment to being in the relationship for the long haul. You make a clear intent to honor yourself and to honor the partner. The same with your children. You will always be their parent, even when they are grown. Your clear intent is to maintain that bond and change along with the changes—to be there no matter what.

A recent survey asked teenagers what they most wanted from their parents. The most common answer? "I want them to be there."

With your friends, both at work and outside of work, it's

the same clear intent. We want our friendships to last. Nobody likes to be thought of as a fair-weather friend. It's clear intent that gives you the energy of being there for people.

Every time you feel insecure, every time there is frustration, anger, or upset, you need to grapple with that so that those issues don't accumulate and undermine the relationship. If you want a long-term positive relationship, whether it's with your partner, your children, your friends, or your colleagues, you have to spend time grappling—taking them on, engaging them in your life.

Throwing rolling waves is a really crucial relationship energy. It's an energy of connection. Making your needs and thoughts known to your loved one and awaiting her response, and having your loved one throw her own rolling waves and awaiting your response—this is the natural rhythm of a good relationship. The image of rolling waves is very useful in intimate relationships because it allows you to see that there need to be spaces in your communication—the rolling in and rolling out.

So often in our relationships we talk over each other.

> Brian, a physician with a very busy practice, arrives home late after having to deal with a hospital emergency. He and his wife, Alison, have tickets to a theater gala that evening. Alison has had her own stressful day. She's a high school teacher and is the track and field coach. After spending an extra hour and a half after school running the team through its relays in preparation for the upcoming track meet, she had to go home and mobilize her own three children to help with dinner. Brian is late, so now the dinner is getting cold.

All Brian wants to do is eat dinner, put his feet up, and watch TV. He does not want to go to the theater.

"Honey, I'm feeling really tired. Why don't you take Melissa [their daughter] to the theater with you tonight instead of me? She really loves seeing live plays."

Alison is rushing around, going through her closet, looking for something to wear. She has started running the shower and calls out from behind the bathroom door, "I think I'll wear the black dress tonight. Your suit is laid out on the bed."

"I've just spoken to Melissa," says Brian, "and she's really happy to go in my place."

"Brian, your ties are behind the closet door. I re-hung them. The striped tie looks good."

"Melissa is studying the play at school. She would really like to see it."

Alison emerges from the bathroom, makeup intact and sweetly perfumed. She looks at Brian and raises her eyebrow in surprise. "You aren't changed for the play."

"I'm not going. Melissa's going with you. I'm too tired to go tonight."

"What? You never said anything about being tired!"

What's happening here? These two have stopped hearing each other—something that happens in many intimate relationships. Brian throws the wave about being tired and doesn't wait for a response. Instead he launches into the second wave about their daughter attending the theater in his place. Alison throws a wave about clothes and straightaway mentions Brian's clothes as well, without waiting for his response. She just makes the assumption that he's getting changed for the theater. Alison misses his wave about Melissa really wanting to go. He is waiting for the return wave of his wife acknowledging his suggestion for a change of plans. Instead he gets another wave about clothing ("You aren't changed for the play"). He tells Alison that Melissa is going instead, and Alison registers both surprise and annoyance, not having heard his very first wave about being tired and not wanting to go to the theater that night. Neither person has given the other time to respond to the rolling wave. They are both focused only on their own waves, their own preoccupations.

One of the facets of communication that is often missed in many of the myriad books about relationship communication is that communication has a rhythm. Make that rhythm too fast (as Brian and Alison did) and the noise of "surf" will drown each other out. Make it too slow and you'll also feel the person hasn't heard you. In other words, waves that are either too fast or too slow will have exactly the same effect— the feeling of not being heard.

Well-timed rolling waves are even more important in parenting. Rolling waves is an excellent energy with children. It allows you to really listen to your child as you wait for her wave to come to you and then recede before you respond with your own wave. That's much better than the time-honored parental knee-jerk reaction to what our kids say and do. We say "no" before we've even heard the request. We say, "Oh, you'll get over it," when we haven't really heard that our daughter just got dumped by a best friend.

Rolling waves can bring you into the rhythm of time and tides in a relationship. I often say that relationships are not so much a journey as they are a flow of energy, an energy loop, if you will, punctuated by both high and low tides.

What about the whirlwind in intimate relationships? It happens, for instance, when we're hit by the great rush of energy known as "falling in love." Courtship, romance, sexual attraction—these are times when relationship energy feels like a whirlwind. Looking back on the whirlwind romances of our past, especially the ones that didn't work out, we often can see how a dose of attentive curiosity would have helped! But you know what they say about hindsight—it's always 20/20. When you're in the grip of the whirlwind, you couldn't care less about 20/20!

There are whirlwind times in parenthood, too. Many women feel it when their children are born, with that dramatic relentless forward-moving contraction of the human body bringing a new life into the world. And then there's the moment for both parents of taking the baby home and all the chaos of sleepless nights and round-the-clock care that unleashes itself into our heretofore precious routines.

Ideally, the whirlwind gradually should give way to the calmer energy of rolling waves, punctuated in marriage and parenthood and friendship by lots of grappling and undulation and shored up by attentive curiosity and clear intent.

Handling the Loss of a Relationship

Grappling with a relationship can sometimes take us to its dissolution. Situations can be so stubbornly conflictual—despite all the best practice of the six energies—that all you can do is call a halt. The warrior of merit knows when to leave the battlefield. It's not a decision taken lightly. It's a decision that hurts deeply. Even when you know that dissolving a relationship is the best thing to do, you will feel it as a loss. And with loss comes grief.

So too when the loss of a loved one is due to death. Both death and divorce are endings, and there is a grieving process. When you're in the middle of grief, this is not the time for an immediate application of the six energies. These are the times when the Shadow Warrior must withdraw into the cave of his being to nurse the wounds, to cry the tears, to feel the hurt, to ache with the loss.

Instead of trying to strategize your way out of your feelings, you form a relationship with your loss. When you have the warrior mind, you form a relationship with the parts of the self you don't show to others, the parts of yourself that contain loss and grief.

> Two weeks after the sudden death of her husband from a heart attack, Donna is back at work. She is known as a cheerful person. To her fellow staff members, she appears her usual jovial self. In fact, she seems so upbeat that people fear to ask her how she's coping at home because they don't want to bring down her mood. After another two weeks of this almost frantic cheerfulness, Donna is combing her hair in the bathroom at lunch break, looks into the mirror, and bursts into tears. She weeps inconsolably as two staff members who just happened to be in the bathroom, attempt to console her. The grief has caught up with her. There are times when the mask of "putting on a brave face" just won't work.

Sometimes you have to take a moratorium from acting as if nothing is wrong. It's a strange society we have that expects people to grieve only for a short period of time and then "get back to normal." How much grief do we shove underground? Why do we not give ourselves the time to grieve? In his book *Ghost Rider*, musician and author Neil Peart described the long motorcycle journey he took after the deaths of his wife and daughter. In the emptiness and desolation of grief, Peart got onto his motorcycle, using the long stretches of road to carry his grief over miles and miles until he had felt it all. He withdrew from normal life for a time. Only then did healing come.

Eventually there comes a time when you find you can distance your heart just a bit from the circumstance. Then you can bear to look at where you are. It's often our close friends and loved ones who help us to do this, who give us the loving space and the nurturing support to face our feelings. We learn to hold our grief in gentleness and not to beat ourselves up for being in grief. And as you allow yourself to be attentive to your grief and the grieving process, it begins slowly to ease.

Here is the best way I have ever found as a warrior to come to terms with that emotional experience. It's not an easy way but it is effective, a way born of the Warrior Mind we have been talking about throughout this book:

> *Gaze right into the heart of your grief with the clarity of mind that lets you know that you can bear it. Do not flinch; do not run away in your heart or mind. Just look at it. When you look directly at your grief and see your loss as one more experience in the ebb and flow of the tides in your life, you will be giving your mind strength to not have to continually relive what happened.*

You can honor grief, you can remember a memory, you can cherish all the good that was in the relationship, you can miss the person—all that is not the same thing as reliving it. You can really only live an experience once, and then it's gone—gone into the realm of memory, where it forms part of your character, part of what makes you continually evolve as *you*.

Unresolved grief keeps you stuck in the past. By looking attentively within yourself at your grief and undulating around it, you bring those feelings into the present awareness so that unhealed wounds will not burden your future.

There is no easy methodology for dealing with the loss of a loved one. But if you are living your life with a sense of presence in the now, if you are grounded in the present moment, your heart and spirit can move back and forth between the memories and the future, between the pain and the joy, between the hopes and the fears, between vulnerability and courage—all converging in this moment we call the present.

That's the secret of relationships—this sense of being in the present. The present is the alchemy that continually transforms our relationships, taking them from birth to life path to death and back to birth again.

A big part of being in the present is the sense of being in your own body. And so in the next chapter, we're going to deal with the body. We're going to talk about using the six energies in defending your body and your personal space so that you feel at home in your body and do not project yourself as a victim. The six energies understood in your mind can, with practice, translate into skills for using your body more effectively in potential self-defense situations and in defining your boundaries. These energies will help you gain a greater sense of your own personal presence and will help you feel safer. We all reside in our bodies and our physical presence is the medium that carries all our interactions with the people and the environments around us.

Reminders to Your Warrior Mind

1. In relationships, your starting point is always your relationship with yourself. The six energies can help you discover a lot about yourself. You may find that one or two of the six energies are more dominant in your personality than the rest of them. Ponder the "energy types" in this chapter to help you identify which type you are.

2. There is no doubt that long-term relationships require a constant juggling act of your needs and desires versus the other person's needs and desires. There is a huge challenge in having another person in your life whose life changes along with yours, and not always in the same direction! Part of the Shadow Warrior mind-set on relationships is to accept that relationships change over time and that all your relationships will go through cycles.

3. One of the greatest relationship traps is projection—our unconscious desire to have our partner, child, or friend be someone we want him or her to be, rather than who he or she truly is. In relationships, as in everything else in terms of the six energies, the fallback position is attentive curiosity, an openness to see and understand what is there. It is hard to do this in an intimate relationship. Intimate relationships are full of projections and one way we can liberate ourselves from these false projections is through seeing our relationships reflected in the six energies.

4. One of the facets of communication in relationships that is often missed is that it has a rhythm. If the rhythm is too fast, the noise of the "surf" will drown each other out. If it's too slow, you'll feel the person hasn't heard you or that you're not making progress. Well-timed rolling waves work really well in marriage and also in parenting.

5. When our relationships become continually conflictual, it may be time to accept dissolution. The warrior of merit knows when to leave the battlefield, even though in intimate and emotional situations, it is very painful to do so. Even more so, we sink into grief when a loved one dies. When you are in the middle of grief, this is not a time for an immediate application of the six energies. These are the times when a Shadow Warrior must withdraw into the cave of his or her being to cry the tears, feel the hurt, and ache with the loss.

6. Instead of trying to strategize your way out of your feelings, form a relationship with your loss. Gaze right into the heart of your grief and hold this in your present awareness. If you are living your life with a sense of presence in the now, your heart and spirit can move back and forth between the memories and the future, between the pain and the joy—all converging in this moment we call the present.

CHAPTER 7

Carrying Yourself Like a Shadow Warrior

One of the dictionary definitions of self-defense is: "The act of defending one's person when physically attacked, by countering blows or overcoming an assailant."

If that's the entirety of what self-defense is thought to be, then I beg to differ. There is much more to it than that. Self-defense is not just physical. It is often psychological, and even spiritual. That makes sense, because we often feel overwhelmed or are intimidated by people or situations where there is no hint of physical threat. We are called on to defend ourselves but may not raise a finger in doing so.

Although this chapter deals with aspects of physical self-defense, including the use of body language, it focuses on how the basis of self-defense lies in the mind and isn't just what your body does.

It's important to stress at the outset that you cannot learn physical self-defense from reading a book. The physical aspects of self-defense are best learned with a qualified instructor over several weeks or months, or, for the totally committed, years. If you do take such training, you may find yourself being more comfortable with the idea of standing up to harassment at work. You'll be able to avoid that confrontation with a drunk in a bar or a mouthy individual on the street. If your child is studying self-defense, she may avoid being bullied in the school yard. In fact, the more prepared you are for a possible confrontation, the less likely you will actually have a confrontation. Proper self-defense training builds self-confidence by honing your skills and fitness levels.

But self-defense, whether physical or psychological, is first of all about cultivating an *awareness*. It's an awareness that you may, at some points in your life, be called on to do serious battle. That battle could involve your body in a physical engagement. Or your mind, in facing a legal or work challenge. Or your heart, in dealing with personal, family, or friendship situations. All this means that you need an attitudinal understanding of what self-defense really is.

Your Best Weapon: Your Mind

In self-defense, what are you responsible for? You are responsible for you. You must be totally aware of how you are acting and reacting. Even when you are defending others, your family, or colleagues, or you have come to the aid of someone being attacked, your responsibility is still toward why you're there and how you handle yourself.

Number one in the arsenal of martial artists is that you do not use your physical skills of self-defense unless you absolutely have to. The point is that there is a time and a place and you choose it. How do you choose it? How do you know whether a physical self-defense situation may present itself? By continually falling back on the first of the six energies—an attentive curiosity—the awake, aware mind of the Shadow Warrior.

Often we just don't see a threat coming our way and are taken by surprise. Or, on the other hand, we do see the potential threat and we ignore it, as in, "Oh, I know I shouldn't be walking alone in a seedy neighborhood late at night, but I'll do it anyway. Nothing will happen to me." Or, at the other end of the spectrum, we see "threats" everywhere and overreact, kind of like the guy in a bar who will start a fight because someone "looked at him wrong."

So you have to learn to use your mind effectively. Is the situation really a threat or is it just noise? If it really is a threat and you are in command of your mind and therefore of your reactions, you can take an action that may totally confuse your opponent. Remember that the first three martial arts principles of confrontation are avoid, confuse, dissuade.

> I recall being in a bar one night where one of the customers, having had too much to drink, was becoming increasingly loud and obnoxious. Soon the guy was getting really offensive, beginning to challenge other people to a fight. When the bartender asked him to leave, the man became angry and began shaking his fist, saying, "Make me!"
>
> For some strange reason, the bouncer was nowhere to be found. I don't know, maybe he had gone to the bathroom. But an elderly gentleman who had been sitting at a nearby table stood up, walked up to the agitated man, and quietly said, "May I help you?"
>
> The obnoxious bar customer was completely taken aback. He had no idea where to take this interaction. He was looking for a confrontation, brewing for a fight, and what he got was an older man in his viewfinder.
>
> The elderly man just stood there in quiet calmness. He did not appear flustered or afraid. Everyone in the

bar watching this was afraid for him. I remember think-ing, "Maybe I should intervene because the old guy could get the crap beaten out of him." But something in the demeanor of the old man signaled to me that he did not need any help, that he was completely in con-trol of the situation.

This man knew how to take the wind out of his op-ponent's sails with a simple four-word question spoken in a gentle manner. The flustered younger man backed away, mumbling an apology, and very shortly thereafter left the bar.

What was the skill of the older man? How did he confuse and dissuade the aggressive drunken cus-tomer? What did he convey that caused the younger man to back off, and not only that, to apologize? Very simple—the older man was completely comfortable in his own body, completely at peace with his own being, and it showed in his body language. The younger man knew instinctively that if he were to hit the older man, he would look like nothing more than a nasty thug who beats up elderly people, and that's not what he was. He was simply a young guy who had had too much to drink. The dignity of the old man repelled the younger man's aggression by making the younger man aware of the image that he did not want to project. In other words, the younger man was outflanked by the older man's emotional composure and self-assurance.

Victim-Proofing Your Body Language

What does your body language convey about you? Do you project "victim"? Do you project "worrywart" with your face lined with concern? Do you project "uptight"? Or do you project warrior—calm warrior, peacemaking warrior, peacekeeping warrior—like that elderly man at the bar?

Predators look for easy marks. They seek out those who are easily perceived as weak, submissive, and unlikely to fight back. Any sign of strength or defiance in their prey is often reason enough for them to rule out that person as a victim.

Go stand in front of a mirror right now and look at the person looking back at you. Are your shoulders hunched, or is your posture straight? What does your face look like? Are your brows furrowed, your mouth in a thin line? Do you look wary or open? Do you stand tall or slouch toward the floor? When you look at yourself do you immediately judge yourself for everything you think is wrong with your body? "I'm too fat, too thin, not muscular enough, losing my hair; I don't have a good figure; my nose is too big."

When you judge yourself as inadequate in your own body, that is going to translate into your body language. Come on, folks, what does it really matter whether you look like some magazine model? Those photos have all been airbrushed and lit to look a certain way. In reality, most people don't look like that. So part of learning to have a good sense of physical presence is to accept your body *and* to accept your mind.

There's a story told about the Dalai Lama that he once was listening to a group of people complain about all the things that were wrong in their lives. Taking all this in, he commented to one of his North American hosts, "These people really don't like themselves." He was truly surprised at this, because from his Buddhist perspective humans should be compassionate toward themselves.

So you start by accepting yourself the way you are. It's not your physical characteristics that can arouse your confident inner warrior; it's your mind that does this. Your mental posture determines your physical posture. Have you ever heard people say about someone who is very small in stature, "He may be small but he walks like he is ten feet tall!" And have you ever seen a person who might tower over you, yet you feel he is rather insubstantial and you have trouble even remembering the encounter? It's as if he was trying to shrink himself—and succeeded.

If you walk slightly hunched over and pulled into yourself, you project "victim"; you project vulnerability. If you are nervous and twitchy, with your eyes darting back and forth, and you are speaking rapidly or breathlessly, seemingly full of nervous energy, you are projecting "victim."

Here's an interesting wrinkle on this, though. An aggressor looking for a victim not only deciphers such victim behaviors, but he can also detect false confidence. So people who tell you that one way not to be a victim is to walk like a puffed-up proud peacock are not giving you good advice.

People selected by predators as victims tend to have a stride that's either too short or too long. Nonvictims, on the other hand, have a smooth and natural gait. How do truly confident people walk? Purposefully. Their posture is erect and their shoulders are back. They appear aware of everything going on around them. They place their attention on whatever is necessary for them to focus on. They look like they are going somewhere. They do not walk in a hurried manner, and even when they do need to hurry, there is a purposefulness to their movements, not a frantic rushing around like the rabbit in *Alice in Wonderland* ("I'm late, I'm late, for a very important date!").

The body language of a warrior is not the John Wayne guns-ablazing body language. That kind of swagger is for movies, for dramatic effect. That stuff is not about real life. Bogus warrior types who do that kind of swaggering in real life will not garner much respect, let alone win any battles. If they are martial artists, that kind of behavior will get them chewed out by the Sensei of their particular martial arts discipline.

Here's an example of the quiet confidence of the Shadow Warrior. It happened when I was getting on a streetcar in the city of Toronto. I happened to have Master Hatsumi's card with me, which had his credentials on it. Another man got on the streetcar and sat on a seat at a right angle to me, just five feet away. I observed him with an attentive curiosity, because I enjoy people watching, whether I'm traveling or just sitting in a café.

As this man sat down, he glanced toward where I was sitting. The glance was quick but it was not cursory. It was clear to me how he immediately took in everything around him. He was not tall but his body language projected a message that this was a man comfortable in himself. He was very quiet, an elderly man with wisps of gray hair. For the untrained eye, it would be easy to overlook him, which is not a mistake I was prepared to make with him.

My fellow passenger was of absolute interest to me. The way he sat, the way he held himself—I knew I was in the presence of another highly trained martial artist, certainly much more advanced than I was, because of his years of experience. Then I looked at his hands, and I was even more certain of my assessment.

I did something I normally would not do. I took Sensei Hatsumi's card and placed it on the seat beside the man. He glanced down, picked it up, looked at it, looked at me. A faint smile crossed his face and he nodded to me. I wanted him to know that I knew what he was. He got off the streetcar four or five blocks later. Our paths never crossed again but in those few moments I saw him for what he was and he didn't have to say a thing. I had picked a subtle way of communicating to him that I was on his wavelength. And he acknowledged that I was correct without speaking a word. I don't even know if he spoke English. He had what I call the warrior confidence.

The warrior confidence is where you first acknowledge that you are fully human. You know that you are vulnerable to the ups and downs of life and the daily challenges that are thrown at you. You're not a warrior by pretending to be superhuman. On the contrary, you are a warrior by knowing and acknowledging that your humanness will lead you into all kinds of finite situations, and that you're ready for them. You neither resist nor attack. You walk a path guided by your own center. You feel present to yourself and in the moment. This includes experiencing the wonder of the fragrance of flowers carried on the wind and all the gentler parts of life, not just the battle parts, not just the competitive parts. Your mental stature is one of attentive curiosity, of awakeness. You are ready to deal with whatever comes your way, even something that totally blindsides you—although in a sense you can never be blindsided when you are in this state of awareness.

Using Attentive Curiosity to Detect Danger and Avoid Panic

If you're in a crowd or a public place and there is somebody around who means you harm, how do you know that? If someone is checking you out as a possible mugging opportunity, how can you be aware of that ahead of time?

When you're in an environment with strangers, for example, in a hotel lobby or a rush-hour crowd, you need the habit of periodically scanning what's happening around you. And if anything you see gives you a tingle of discomfort, a slight feeling that something is amiss, trust that feeling and get moving. It doesn't matter whether it makes sense or not. Just move.

Now you may ask, "What's the difference between having attentive curiosity and scanning the environment, and being paranoid and scared of your own shadow?" The difference is that when you're scanning your environment, you are doing so from a place of calm awareness, not of skittish nervousness. Your mind is focused on just looking around. You're not looking around with the expectation of finding something bad. You're not looking around for reasons to interpret the environment as scary. You're simply looking around to see what's there.

If what's there is making you uncomfortable, pay attention to that with your energies of attentive curiosity and awareness. If someone across the street is leering at you and starts to cross the street toward you, move out of there. Don't wait around to find out if this person really means to do you harm.

The projection of a warrior is not one that's loaded with weapons, looking for trouble and spoiling for a fight. The projection of a warrior is a sense of quiet and purposeful presence, the projection that you are a person who goes about your own business and that you do not expect anyone to interfere with you.

When you scan properly, you go on to learn to take reasonable precautions.

I remember a time some years ago when my wife and I

were driving through a town in New Hampshire late at night. We managed to get ourselves lost, so we decided to stop to ask for directions at a convenience store. There was a small group of young men congregating around the door.

I cautioned my wife, "I want you to lock all the doors." This was not done out of paranoia or fear but simply out of caution and common sense.

I walked around the front of the car and said, "Hi, guys, how are you doing? Can you help me out? I'm not from around here and I'm looking to get back toward the highway."

The young men looked at me and I could see they were considering how to respond to me. I stood there very calmly. Finally one of them said, "Yeah, no problem," and gave me directions.

I thanked him and shook his hand, which surprised him, and went back to the car. One of the young men called after me, "Hey, are you some kind of cop or something?"

I said, "Hell, no, just a tourist heading home. I thank you again for your help."

What I projected to them was the demeanor of "I have respect for you, I am polite to you, and I am not afraid of you." Therefore, they had no reason to become aggressive because there was no challenge for them to respond to.

People, especially women, often ask me, "How do I walk down a dark street alone at night?" and my short answer is: "Don't. Don't get yourself into a position where you have to do that. Take a cab or have someone walking with you."

"Okay," the person will sometimes say, "but what if I don't have a choice? What if I really have to walk down that street and don't have anyone with me?"

If you absolutely have to walk down that dark street late at night alone, carry a flashlight with you. Nasty characters who haunt dark streets depend on the darkness for cover. So if you're shining a bright beam of light, that's likely going to discourage them. If you have a cell phone, call a family member or friend to let her know where you are and that you'll call her again when you get to your destination. If she doesn't hear from you within a certain time, she'll know to come look for you or to call for help. This may sound silly, but if you're a woman on a dark street alone, sometimes it pays to be silly in that way.

Let's take the scenario that there really is a guy walking behind you on the street. The person may be following you or he may not be. Don't immediately assume the posture of a victim. Keep your attentive awareness alert and go into caution mode. The first thing to remember is not to stop. If you hesitate in your steps or stop, that's a body language indicator that you're vulnerable and afraid. Change your pattern. Cross to the other side of the street. If he follows you, cross back and see what happens. Do not turn and confront the person. If your instincts tell you the man means you harm, if there are lights on anywhere on the street, do not hesitate to go up to the nearest door and ask for assistance.

As you can see, it's really not a good idea to get yourself into that position in the first place, because if he really wants to attack you, he will. Shining a flashlight, walking quickly and purposefully, crossing to the other side of the street, and banging on someone's door will lessen the danger somewhat, but it won't eliminate it if the person really means you harm.

A friend of mine owns a horse farm. Every night she has to walk out to the barn with her flashlight to make sure the horses are fed, watered, and settled in their stalls for the night. I told her, "Your vulnerability is between the barn and the house in the dark." I advised her to have one of her dogs walk with her at all times, the biggest and most mature of them. In the darkness of the country, a dog will pick up the scent of danger before an untrained human will. So if you're going to have to walk alone in the dark in a rural area, have a dog with you or another person.

If, however, you're in a situation where there are other people around—say, in a mall—and some creepy guy is following you, you may choose to use the whirlwind strategy of confronting the guy in public. You can turn around and say in a voice audible to others, "Are you following me?" or "Can I help you? Why are you following so close behind me?" Only do this if you're fairly sure the guy is following you and is not just some harried shopper who has the misfortune to fall into step behind you.

Another strategy is that you can approach a mall security officer. Just seeing you talking to the officer is usually enough to scare the guy off.

Do *not* attempt the verbal whirlwind confrontation of "Why are you following me?" if there are no other people around.

If you're in a bar or restaurant and you're getting unwanted attention, simply approach the bouncer or the maitre d' and say, "That person is bothering me," and let the bouncer handle it. Don't try to do it yourself. When it's time for you to leave, have the waiter or bouncer call a cab for you and ask him or her to see you to your cab (or to your own car), just in case your spurned suitor is hanging around outside.

Now let's say that you're in a situation where there are other people and you know it's not likely that you'll get stalked or bothered by anyone—for example, at a conference. Even if you're not worrying about "bad guys," you want to know how to use your body language to project self-confidence and calmness. You can do that by walking straight up to people and introducing yourself. Seminars on networking call this "schmoozing" or "working a room," but I bet you didn't think of it as a psychological self-defense technique. It is. If you take the initiative and say to someone, "Hello, how are you? I'm Mary [or I'm Joe]," if anyone has any thoughts of confrontation or mental intimidation, that just neutralizes it—because you're not projecting victim; you're not projecting confrontational structure.

If you have to work a room, scan with your attentive curiosity for the person with the most aggressive body language and introduce yourself to that person. Your making the first move neutralizes that person's aggressive come-on and you have just controlled the energy of that transaction.

SCANNING

I've referred several times to scanning. What exactly is it? Scanning is when you *deliberately* pause to take in your environment. Have you ever seen people upon entering a room pause at the door and look around? That is a power behavior. Do this whether it's a hotel lobby, the boardroom, the cafeteria at work, or a conference room. In that brief instant you're scanning to see who's there and what's going on.

Some people scan to their left and some scan to their right. It doesn't matter which direction you scan first; just do it. And when you scan with an attentive curiosity, just looking to see what's there, your instincts will tell you if anything is amiss. Scan when you go into a parking lot. Scan when you get out of an elevator. Scan before you get into an elevator. If you're a woman and there is just one man in the elevator, it may be a good idea to lean to the side of caution and wait for the next elevator that has several people in it.

In a parking lot or lobby, I scan the vertical supports be-cause those are good hidey-holes for nasty types. Don't walk close to the vehicles, but as close to center as you can get. If you're sitting in a hotel lobby waiting for someone, sit near the center, not off to the side, where someone could accost you. If you're alone in a bar, sit near the bartender. If you're working late at night, have the night security guard accompany you to your car.

Many of these suggestions will be more applicable to women than men, simply because of the fact that women are more vulnerable to physical attack. However, men can also get mugged or be put in danger by nasty types in a bar or on the street, so the scanning abilities are equally important to them, in my opinion.

The Undulation Move in Self-Defense

Undulation is one of the best moves in physical self-defense you can ever learn. It's a wonderful motion of dropping down, either to the right or to the left, and around, and it does not depend on your physical strength. If you find yourself physi-cally grabbed by someone, this move gives you the ability to get out of the entrapment.

I remember once watching a dojo trainee working with a senior instructor who had the trainee in a very strong hold. This being a brand-new martial arts trainee, he didn't have any experience with releasing techniques. He tried every World Wrestling Entertainment move known. Nothing worked until finally he was guided by another instructor to use a body mo-tion of easy escape, the move I have come to call the technique of undulation.

How best to describe the physical undulation move? It is a full-body movement but it starts from the hips down to the feet and up to the shoulders. Consider the hips as the center. If the center moves to the left, the shoulders have to follow. If it moves to the right, the shoulders follow. If you're twisting around, both the center and the shoulders rotate. One begins to follow the other and this is how we learn to use the whole body in self-defense.

Here's how you use undulation techniques to release the grip of someone who has grabbed you from behind. First, drop your weight straight down, and as you do, move your hips to the right or left away from your attacker's center and continue dropping your body weight toward the floor. This is going to make it very difficult for the attacker to hold on to you.

Here's a way to practice this. Have a friend grab hold of your belt from behind. Drop down, moving sideways away from your friend's centerline of balance. This is going to give you a good sense of how undulation feels. Most attackers from the back will grab you around the top part of your body and try to pin your arms. You're going to redistribute your weight by dropping your weight toward the floor and moving your hips away from the attacker sideways, which will enable you to begin lifting your arms from your shoulders outward as your opponent's grip loosens as you are moving toward the floor. You will quickly see that your hands and your elbows are now free to strike toward your opponent's groin.

I have done this move with professional martial artists and I've done it with total beginners and with people who have no intention of becoming martial artists. Once they get the sense that the whole body moves at the same time, led first by the gravity of the body dropping down and then by the hips, they can see it's almost impossible for another person to hold them fast.

Have you ever seen a toddler having a temper tantrum in a shopping mall? The distraught parent usually picks up the child from behind. And what does the child do? The child drops his or her body weight toward the floor and moves to the side, and for a moment the parent almost loses the grip on the child. That's the undulation move. Children know it instinctively. And you see variations of it in demonstrations such as protest marches, where the protesters turn their body weight into dead weight so that the security forces can't lift them up very well. What they're usually missing, however, is the movement of the hips. If they added the hip movement, the "protest move" would be much more effective.

The undulation move can also be used if the attacker grabs you from the front. You still drop your weight straight down and your hips go to the side—it's the same move. From the front, though, you also have the advantage of forehead meets chin, forehead meets nose, knee meets groin. So you could also strike your opponent in one of those vulnerable areas as you are undulating.

Remember what attackers cannot protect. They cannot protect their throat. They cannot protect their nose. They cannot protect their chin. They cannot protect their eyes. They cannot protect their groin. They cannot protect their knees. So a sharp strike to any of those areas will come as a shock to them and temporarily weaken their ability to hold on to you.

However, my advice is not to try to be like some street thug who likes to throw punches. The idea of the undulation move is to break the attacker's hold and buy you time to run. You are not trying to get into hand-to-hand combat with your opponent. If in your undulation move you've been able to drive your elbow into your attacker's groin (ouch!) as you drop your weight toward the ground, don't hang around looking to deliver more blows. You are not karate expert Jackie Chan!

The purpose of the undulation move is for you to break the grip and gain time to move away from the attacker, taking advantage of the fact that the attacker will be confused by having the grip broken so easily and will need a few seconds to recover and continue his aggression. *Your* job is to run like hell to get out of there!

A Body-Language Variation on Undulation

We've been talking about how to use undulation in the event of a physical attack. But the reality is that for most readers of this book, being physically attacked will not be a common occurrence. Hopefully you will not have to use the undulation move to get away from an attacker. But if someone does attack you, then it's a move you can use to break the grip and increase your chance of escape.

Is there a way that a physical undulation-type move can help us break the psychological grip of another person in our daily lives? Can undulation body language be used in an argument or a verbal confrontation or a power struggle? The answer is: Yes, it can.

I sometimes show students an exercise that illustrates how undulation body language can help them take control of a conversation. I tell them to try, when in conversation with another person, to move in a ninety-degree arc to their right. They see that almost 100 percent of the time the other person will stop speaking briefly and will turn to realign himself with the student. I tell my students to then count ten seconds and move back to the original position in a reverse ninety-degree arc, all the while observing the reaction of the other person. My students couldn't get through their stories without much laughter about what happened.

An arguer or verbal confronter relies on eye contact to help maintain power. If you move to the side (undulate), even just slightly, you will break the person's visual hold and he or she will be forced to follow your body language in order to realign body position and take back control of the conversation.

So, if you're having an argument or confrontation with someone, and you're standing, move to the side. And if you're sitting in a chair, get up and move. For example, let's say you're being chewed out by your manager or supervisor and you feel that the chewing out is not justified. You're sitting in a chair opposite the manager. You can undulate by getting up and moving sideways. You can say something like, "Excuse me, I've got a bit of a leg cramp and I just need to stand up for a moment."

The effect on the other person is that the psychological grip—the power in the conversation—has been broken. The mind of the other person will register, "Hey, where did he go?" And so he will stop talking briefly because he doesn't want to be talking to thin air. When the conversation position has been realigned, if you are still not happy with the power dynamics, move back to where you started, forcing the other person to follow you yet again. Keep moving at intervals—but avoid continual pacing and dramatic gestures of walking all the way to the other side of the room. Just move enough so that the person has to shift his body position in order to keep eye contact with you.

This kind of body language undulation breaks the focus of a verbal aggressor. Remember the martial arts ideas of avoid, confuse, dissuade, discussed in the introduction? Your body language of moving slightly to the side is definitely going to confuse your opponent. When your opponent is confused, in that confusion the person can't hang on to aggression or exercise power. The momentary break in the person's focus allows you to begin to turn the energy and the power toward yourself and what you want to say. That's a fundamental principle in the martial arts—blending the opponent's energies with your own.

> An employee of a large bookstore chain was undergoing her annual employee evaluation. The manager said to her, "You spend too much time talking with customers. You are too chatty."
>
> That comment annoyed the employee because she knew that the extra time she spent talking with customers was resulting in more sales than her colleagues were achieving. She replied to the evaluator, "Evidently my ability to chat with customers results in my getting a lot more sales."
>
> The evaluator's response was, "Well, yes, but we have a set policy with our staff that you're only supposed to spend a certain amount of time with each customer and move on as quickly as possible."
>
> The employee then wanted to argue: "If I have a customer who comes in to buy one book, and because of a conversation with me, he ends up buying four books, that extra time is worth it, is it not?"
>
> So what happened here is that the employee and the manager have now gotten themselves into a conflict over their interpretation of customer service. As long as the employee stays seated in the chair, energy-

wise the conflict is weighted in favor of the manager. If, however, the employee were to say something like, "I just need to stand up a minute to stretch," and then move slightly to the side, the aggressor's energy would be temporarily broken. Standing up to move about a bit would not be interpreted as hostile or confrontational. But it will effectively break the other person's total concentration, and so when the employee begins to give her interpretation of events, she will have a better chance that the other person may begin to respond to her more flexibly and less rigidly.

In a power struggle type of conversation, you can't equalize that power until the hold is broken, just as when you are physically grabbed you can't take back your power until you have physically escaped from the hold. In verbal disagreement, you may not end up getting everything you want, but by breaking the energy hold, you will more likely get *some* of what you want and often *a lot* of what you want. And you will have done so not by making the other person feel defeat (which would make the person defensive), but by making the person reevaluate the energy of the situation and allowing in new energies.

Next time you hear a keynote speech, observe the speaker's movements. Who is likely to arouse your interest more—the one who just stays put in one place behind the lectern or the one who occasionally moves aside from the lectern in both directions? The moving speaker gets the audience to follow his or her energy. The stationary speaker sends out energy in only one direction. The moving speaker is multidirectional. That's mental undulation accompanied by "undulation" body language. And it works.

Clear Intent in Self-Defense Body Language

The issue about clear intent is never to lose the focus of choosing to act in your own best interest. Acting in your own best interest is not the same thing as being selfish or not considering others' needs. I am using the phrase in the context of doing what you need to do to keep yourself safe and empowered so that you can be the best you can be in every situation in your life. When you are the best you can be, then your efforts to help others and to create harmony with others will be that much more powerful and effective.

So, the key to not being a victim of other people's agendas, whether physical or psychological, is to decide that you will under no circumstances be a victim. That's right—it's a decision. It doesn't matter if you've been a victim in the past. It doesn't matter if last week you didn't handle a conflict well at work or in your relationships. It doesn't matter if someone in the past got the better of you. You can decide *right now* that you've had it with being a victim and you can form a clear intent to be an inner warrior instead.

That intent will then give birth to the clear intent of every action you take. In a physical self-defense situation, your clear intent is going to be to get out of there. In a verbal or psychological opposition situation, your intent may be to get out, but it would more likely be to shift the energy toward a more empowering and less anxious position for yourself. Even if you don't win the argument totally, you will still feel inwardly more confident because you will have taken control of your own energies and not have allowed yourself to just be pushed around by others.

If you're in a situation where you suspect someone will talk down to you, you can signal a clear intent of equalizing power by putting yourself in a position where you will not be physically "one down." For example, if the person walks up to your desk, just stand up. By standing up, and shifting your position ever so slightly to either side, you devictimize your posture, signaling your intent that you are going to address the confronter from a position of strength.

Grappling in Self-Defense

Overall, using the next three energies in a physical sense ideally involves some training. Grappling is not difficult but it does take practice, and you do need to be *shown* the techniques. In this chapter, all I can do is describe some of the salient points, but I highly recommend that if you want to know more about physical grappling, you take some training in self-defense.

If you're in a physical self-defense situation, how do you grapple? In our Western society we assume that in a physical conflict the person who is lying on the ground has been knocked down and that that is a submissive position. But in many martial traditions, that is soon revealed as a fallacy. For many who are trained in the martial arts, especially those that involve skilled grappling, such as Judo, down on the ground is one of their preferred positions to fight.

And here's the reason: When you're on the ground, it is very difficult for your opponent, who is standing up, to reach down and strike you with her hands. Therefore she has to kick you. When you're down and your opponent tries to kick you, you still have your feet, your knees, your elbows, your hands, and your head all available to you as weapons. And what really stands out about the on-the-ground grappling position is that the opponent's vulnerable groin area is very close to your fists, much closer than if you were standing up. Your feet can do a terrible number on an opponent's groin or knees from the ground. And you can strike with a more accelerated force if you're on the ground.

Here is an exercise anyone can do. A friend of mine called Rick is a skilled boxer. Often when we went to lunch he would talk about boxing exercises and I would talk about grappling techniques on the mat. I invited him to the dojo. I told him I was going to show him a technique that I bet he didn't know. I got down on my knees and had him do the same, facing me. Then I invited him to grip my wrists. Here's the cardinal rule of gripping the wrists: Once you grip them, don't let go. All you have to do is, without getting off your knees and without releasing the wrists, take that person down on the mat so that his shoulders are pinned. My friend was surprised to find that even with all his strength and athleticism and being half my age, once he had hold of my wrists, he could grapple me down to the mat but could not pin me for the required three count. The more committed he became to using his muscle strength, the more fatigued he became with the struggle. He became winded, was drenched in sweat, and could not continue the exercise. A person using muscle strength will fatigue must faster than a grappling opponent who has learned how to use his whole body for leveraging, through proper breathing and technique.

For starters, try this on a safe mat against someone who is roughly your own physical size. Try to keep him there while counting one thousand and one, one thousand and two, one thousand and three. If the person's shoulder lifts from the mat before the three count is over, you have to start again from the kneeling position. Try it, but don't get too rambunctious with each other.

A variation of this is to place the four fingertips of both of your hands under your opponent's wrists. The fingers of your hands should be touching each other with your thumbs on the other side of the wrists. Squeeze with your fingers, using your thumb as leverage to increase your hold. This will weaken your opponent's grip.

Should you hang around to grapple if you're being attacked physically? Hell no, unless you're an expert in self-defense. Use the undulation move to break the hold and get out of there! But if you have to grapple, you'll need some rudimentary CQC (close quarter combat) skills. First, you'll want to come in close with the vulnerability of your opponent. The eye-gouging move is one you can use from down on the ground if the attacker is looming over you, or from a standing position. The move itself is very simple. Just arrange your fingers like the "peace sign" with your index and middle fingers and make like one of the Three Stooges, poking directly into the attacker's eyes. Even if you miss slightly, it will usually distract your opponent long enough for you to run away.

If you're down on the ground, forget about all those television techniques where you see one attacker grabbing another's ankle and trying to pull the other person down. Pulling someone's ankle if that person weighs more than you is not going to result in that person falling backward. Instead, use your foot as a weapon to strike right into the groin or into the shin or kneecap. Go for those vulnerable areas.

If you're not on the ground and you haven't managed to break the hold with undulation, you can try stomping the person's foot. The human foot has many little bones, all of which can be easily damaged. If your attacker's ability to walk is hampered, the attacker cannot chase after you very effectively.

What do you do if your attacker has a weapon? That's a

whole different ball game, folks. Do *not* try to take down an opponent who is pointing a knife at you. In that kind of situation, try to get something in between you and the opponent. For example, take off your coat and hold it in front of you. Hold your briefcase in front of you, or your purse.

Another thing to know if you're down on the ground is to keep rolling. Roll and strike. If your opponent is standing over what he perceives to be a victim, imagine his surprise if the "victim" rolls and strikes hard with the foot. Keep moving.

Rolling Waves: The Idea of Continual Movement

If you are trying to follow the advice to keep moving but you are unable to get away, you may throw a strike to the kneecap. Then, as your attacker crouches over in pain, you roll in again by bringing your knee to his temple. You don't do the wait and see thing if you're under serious attack. You just go from one wave to the next wave to the next and the next until you escape and get out of there.

For example, the rolling wave is when you try to get to the foot and your opponent moves and you miss. You keep going—perhaps coming up on your knees and throwing your knee into your opponent's opposite knee and trying to buckle it. Follow that with a kick to the thigh and then a kick to the groin. You put your foot down and come back with another kick to the knee. An advanced technique is to roll into the opponent, using your legs as a whip. As you're rolling out, you're then bringing the leg across and using your heel as a weapon.

Facility with these kinds of moves, however, *does* take training. But it's remarkable how even a short series of self-defense lessons can make you quite effective in fighting if you have to.

The Whirlwind

If you have to pull out all the stops, when you're fighting for your life, become as fierce as you can possibly be. Make a lot of noise. Strike, scratch, bite, kick, roar—all targeted against your opponent. The whirlwind is the acceleration of rolling waves. These types of moves, as I've said above, do require training and are not things you can learn from reading a book.

Having said that, as a general guideline to follow, let me tell you a story that involved a friend of mine named Ron who used the whirlwind in a much more simplified and direct manner.

> I was with Ron and several of his buddies in a pub where a loudmouth was trying to trash talk one of his group into a fistfight. There were about fourteen men divided down the middle in this potential conflagration. I didn't know any of the guys except Ron, but I did know that we were confident we would be victorious if push came to shove.
>
> Ron is the kind of guy who would rather party and be nice to one and all. But he walked over to the troublemaker and threw one punch upside his head, whereupon Mr. Loudmouth became Mr. Closedmouth.
>
> Silence prevailed in the whole room. Then Ron simply walked back to what he was doing without saying a word.
>
> That's the whirlwind in its most basic form. The

loud, aggressive guy got his ticket punched by someone who decided enough was enough, bringing to an end the possibility of a much greater altercation.

Ron is a peacemaker who is six element qualified. He's just the type of man who likes to preempt trouble by going straight to the whirlwind. I don't recommend this as your major energy move. But there are times when it is the only thing that will restore balance to a situation. Use sparingly, and hopefully not at all.

Your Number One Inner Safety Strategy

With physical self-defense, your primary strategies should be, first, not to carry yourself like a victim; second, to prevent yourself from getting into situations where you could be physically confronted (for example, avoiding unlit dark streets late at night in nasty neighborhoods); and, third, if you are confronted physically, to focus primarily on breaking the opponent's hold through a simple undulation move and then get out of there as fast as you can.

Many people find self-defense training to be empowering, and there does seem to be a psychological spillover in that when you learn some basic self-defense techniques, you will begin to alter your body language. If self-defense training is of interest to you, there are many ways to find resources in your community. Many martial arts dojos offer modified programs aimed only at basic self-defense for nonmartial artists.

But your number one inner safety strategy physically is your own body language—how you carry yourself. Having a warrior consciousness involves both thought and motion. Thought + Motion = No Room for Fear.

Reminders to Your Warrior Mind

1. Physical self-defense is not just learning to counter physical blows if you are attacked. Physical self-defense is, paradoxically, first a mental discipline. It's important to stress here that you cannot learn physical self-defense from merely reading a book. If you are interested in learning more about self-defense, seek out what your community may have to offer in terms of resources and training programs.

2. Your body language plays a crucial role in self-defense. Do you project "victim"? Do you project "worrywart"? Do you project "uptight"? Or do you project warrior mind—calm warrior, peacemaking warrior, peacekeeping warrior? You start by accepting your body exactly as you are. And then you work on your mental "posture." Your mental posture determines your physical posture.

3. One of the most effective uses of attentive curiosity in self-defense situations is the practice of scanning. Always when entering a new environment, or even a more familiar one, pause to scan what is there. You're not looking around with the expectation of finding something bad. You're simply looking to see what's there. When you enter a room, pause at the door and look around. That is a power behavior. Do this whether it's a hotel lobby, the boardroom, the cafeteria at work, or a conference room. In that brief scanning you can learn a lot about what's going on, what the vibes are in that environment.

4. Undulation is one of the best moves in physical self-defense you can ever learn. It's a motion of dropping down,

either to the right or to the left, and around, and it does not depend on your physical strength. The undulation allows you to break the hold of someone who has you in a grip.

5. There is an excellent body-language variation on undulation that can help you break the psychological "grip" of another person. When you wish to take control of the energy flow of a conversation, negotiation, or confrontation, move physically slightly to the side of the person you are talking to, forcing him or her to follow your movement. This kind of body-language move breaks the focus of a verbal aggressor and allows you to turn the energy toward yourself and what you want to say or do.

6. There are many effective and easy grappling moves you can learn in physical self-defense. Several are described in this chapter, but realistically you should consider doing some self-defense training if you want to be an effective grappler. Rolling waves and the whirlwind, used physically in self-defense, also require some training. But the good news is that it doesn't have to be a long period of training. Most people can learn to use the six energies effectively in physical self-defense within a relatively short time.

_____

CHAPTER 8

Living a More
Powerful Life

At those times in our lives when we feel under siege, why do many of us turn toward the spiritual? Why do we begin asking questions about meaning? It's because when we perceive that we're beyond our own capacities and beyond our limits, we look for a source larger than ourselves to give us the energy and the strength to get through the challenging situation.

The Spiritual

By "spiritual" I am not talking about specific religions or belief systems. What I'm referring to is the universal human instinct to search for meaning and to draw upon an inspiration bigger than ourselves. Whenever we're having challenges in our lives, whether large or small, we don't want to feel that our own little energy system is all there is.

Among the many prayers used by Alcoholics Anonymous

is a very simple and succinct one that can apply to all of us as we live our lives:

Oh Lord, help me to remember that nothing is going to happen to me today that you and I together can't handle.

In the human condition we seem to need that sentiment. We need to feel that there is nothing we can't handle. That feeling plays a role in helping us develop a sense of inner safety. If you feel that you can draw upon energies that will help you handle anything, whether you call that energy God, or inspiration, or hope, or higher self, or philosophy, you will feel safer in your own skin. In the sense that we all yearn for our lives to have some kind of meaning and purpose, we are all spiritual.

As you walk your life's path, I guarantee you that the end of that path is death. That's a hard fact many of us don't want to acknowledge. Between now and your death, you are faced with making many decisions. The decisions you make reflect your values, your struggles, your hopes, dreams, fears, desires, goals, mistakes, and accomplishments—all of which make up the story known as "your life."

Many times in my practice of the martial arts I have struggled with a mind-set of trying to overcome a difficulty. And then all of a sudden there would come a moment when something inside me just relaxed and I was perfectly aware of where I was supposed to be. The understanding that I was trying to come to terms with just fell into place. It wasn't triggered by any specific event. It was more like an inner letting go of struggle. I had gotten in touch with the energy flow in my body and mind. The idea of energy is very important to the martial arts. If you block the energy flowing through you, you will not be an effective fighter. So on the larger scale, if you block the energy flowing through your whole life, you will not experience your full human capacity.

Some of the most interesting martial artists I've associated with and sparred with were brown belts. These individuals were one step below the black belt. They were totally motivated, totally committed. You didn't have to psych them up in their practice. They were so close to attaining the black belt that they could smell it and taste it. They lived it. They slept it. They walked it. They worked three times as hard for their black than they did for any other level of belt ranking.

A big part of their intent was to do honor to the Sensei by qualifying to wear the black belt in their particular discipline. They knew that these traditions represented an outlook and approach to life that is larger than they were. They knew this every time they grappled. They knew this every time they used rolling waves, every time they got down on the mat. They did their meditations. They did their breathing. They called all their energies together, drawing upon the inspiration of the tradition, the example set by their Sensei, and their own determination to transcend the level of brown belt.

Maybe this process is a form of self-hypnosis. Or a form of self-talk. Or a competitive mind-set. But I think that it's much more than that. When we spend time pursuing something we feel is larger than ourselves, there is a sense of wonder. For most of us, it's not going to be the martial arts that give us the sense of wonder. It might be what we've done in our career, or in raising our children, or in our community involvements, or in what we have done for humanity or to protect the environment.

This sense of wonderment and the seeking of purpose does

not come from our everyday mind, which can be the seed of war, competitiveness, and conflict. Rather it comes from the heart, where you reach out for a sense of connectedness to life. Is that not what spirituality is all about: reaching from the heart, assisting someone when she doesn't necessarily ask for it? Part of the philosophy of the martial arts is to live honorably, to seek and promote peace, and to practice compassion. Any Sensei who does not teach this to his or her students is not worthy of the name.

The Warrior Mind

There is an expression in the martial arts world that says, "The warrior of merit wins the battle without causing others to feel defeat." That's a lot easier said than done. When you're training as a martial artist, you're training to fight. You're training to fight with your body and with your mind. To learn and train in the martial arts, you must come to understand that the way of the warrior means that there might be times in your life when you have to employ the use of your physical or mental skills in combat. And so there will be times when, if you're a skilled fighter, whether physically or psychologically, you will appear to defeat people. We've talked about many of those situations in this book. If you use a physical undulation move to break an attacker's hold, you will certainly defeat the purpose of the attacker. If you use a mental strategy of targeted rolling waves to help you overcome harassment at work, you will defeat the harassment. So it's easy to get lost in the idea of the battle itself and see it in black and white terms of winner and loser.

The warrior mind, however, looks at it in a different way.

When a martial artist trains, what he trains for is to maintain peace. The martial artist learns that overt conflict is the last resort, that you do everything possible to use your energies to redirect negative energies. Your aim is not primarily to defeat an enemy. It is to use the energies in the situation to restore harmony both to yourself and to the environment. True peace-makers actually have to be the ultimate of warriors. They have to know that there is the power to fight at any time but do everything possible to fight in the least destructive way.

When it comes to the conflicts in our lives, we have choices. We can choose to block them out and pretend they aren't there (denial). We can run away (flight). We can stay in our own habitual patterns and with our own small group of people with whom we're comfortable (timidity). We can criticize. We can reject. All these are ways our fears taunt us. And they are ways we use our fears to taunt or reject others.

But we can also choose not to victimize ourselves. We can choose to embrace a larger, more inclusive energy. We can choose to be a peacemaker. In this mode, we never lose touch with our warrior mind. We are always at the ready to defend that which we most love in our lives. All the while, we always have a stance of seeking peace wherever possible.

This reminds me of an occasion two or three summers ago when I was riding my motorcycle. When you're wearing biker leathers and riding, you look much bigger than you actually are. There was an SUV ahead that was making a right turn when its engine quit. I pulled my bike in front of the vehicle, got off, and approached the occupants of the SUV. They turned out to be two men who came from a foreign country. I don't remember now exactly where they came from, only that they had a hard time speaking English. As I walked toward them in my biker gear and sunglasses, I could see that they were nervous. I removed my sunglasses and smiled at them. That broke some of the ice, although they were still looking at each other in a flustered way, not knowing how to interpret my approach. After all, you know how bad bikers are! We want to kill everybody! We want to be nasty and rude and take the people's cars, and so forth! That was no doubt running through their minds.

I recognized what the problem was with the car. The driver had flooded the engine and it had stalled. Using a slower speaking pattern and lots of hand gestures, I was able to get the driver to follow my instructions as to how to get the car started again. Before long I had the throttle and the air filter off, reassembled everything, and gave the driver the signal to start the engine. Did I make friends? No. But I sure as heck made them less fearful of me. That's peacemaking.

I once was asked by a family to teach their sixteen-year-old son, Robert, martial arts because he was getting into trouble at school and they thought that learning the discipline of the martial arts would be good for him, give him something to focus his energies on, and increase his confidence. During our first session together, I asked him, "Do you know what the spirit is?"

He said, "Yeah, that's what happens when you die."

I said, "Okay, but before you die, where is the spirit?"

He answered, "The spirit is in the body."

"So is there spirit in your body?" I asked.

"I don't think so," he replied.

"So it's other people who have a spirit in their body but you don't?" I asked.

He shook his head in some confusion.

What I'm calling "spirit" here is what many Eastern philosophies call "chi"—the life force energy in our bodies and indeed in everything that is alive. And this young man was so out of touch with himself he could not feel his own life force energy. Often a person who is out of touch with his own energy will seek unconsciously to find that energy through aggressive behavior, which is what this young guy was doing in getting into conflict with his teachers and with other kids.

"Okay," I said to him, "we're going to do some physical stuff, and I promise you that I won't ask you to do anything I haven't done myself many times."

I showed him how to do a basic roll. He did the roll, stood back up, and said, "Oh, man, I don't want to do that. That hurts too much."

"You know," I said, "you're not quite human yet."

"I am so," he protested.

"No, you're not, because all you're doing is fuming and whining, and you're not thinking beyond your own needs. You have many gifts and you're not aware of even one of them. So you use your energy to perpetuate negativity in your life. But when doing a roll here on the mat hurts you, that's when you realize you are human. You can be hurt. You know what it feels like. So if you lash out and hurt somebody else, it's going to come back on you. And you know what? On one level you know that already."

A few years later I saw him again. His body had filled out and he was more muscular. He told me how his life was going. He recounted one story about how he was challenged to a street fight and how he had walked away from it.

"Why did you walk away?" I asked.

"Well, the guy who wanted to fight me was drunk and he was half my size. I just couldn't do it."

And I said, "Robert, you've become human. Now you can live your life with confidence. You can walk about without having fear shoved down your throat and without having to attack others. That's what this life is about. But we've all got to get there. Some of us do, and some of us don't. You're on your way."

"Yeah," he said, and nodded.

Robert had begun to live his life with the warrior mind.

Attentive Curiosity Within the Larger Meaning of Your Life

Attentive curiosity in the spiritual sense means looking with eyes that are unfettered or unclouded with misunderstanding, hate, anger, or disgust, or any negative energy. The Zen Buddhist "beginner's mind" comes in here.

The beginner looks at everything as if seeing it for the first time. Try it. Look at things in your life as if you have never encountered the situations before.

Come on, you may say, isn't life about learning from experience? Who wants to look at his car as if he's never seen it before? Who wants to go to a job interview as if he's never been through one before? Who wants to ask for a date as if he's never been through that before? But indeed there *was* a time when you did those things for the very first time. And that's the feeling you need to recover from your memory bank.

Life is indeed about learning from experience. But it's an interesting exercise to just lay all those life experiences aside and practice looking at things and situations and thoughts and feelings with a beginner's mind. A friend of mine used to talk about her son's sixth-grade teacher, who told her students that one way to get a fresh perspective on things is to pretend you're a Martian and you've just landed from Mars. You haven't ever seen anything that's on Earth. How would you explain these things to yourself? How would you describe what you see? How would you explain to the Martians back up on Mars what you saw and heard?

Maybe you would report back to Mars that human beings spend a lot of their time in colorful machines with wheels following a labyrinthine pattern of roads—that they go one way in the morning and the opposite way at night. Maybe you would report that children spend their days in a room with a large board at the front and that the adult in the room writes on the board with a large white stick, and then a bell rings, and everyone runs out into the yard and makes a lot of noise until the next bell, when everyone gets quiet again.

Try it; it's fun. Describe your life to yourself as if you are a Martian who has no clue what you're seeing and try to make sense of it. When you play with attentive curiosity in this way, it actually loosens up your mental chi and leaves you feeling more alert and alive.

When you look at your entire life, at everything that happens, with an attentive curiosity, you find yourself living in the now, in the present moment.

I remember making business calls to a nursing home that bought supplies from the company I was running at the time. I would joke around with the elderly ladies who liked to tell me their stories. One lady had a gleam in her eye and a wicked smile, so I asked her, "So what have you got planned for your future?"

"Well, young man," she declared, "I'm going where you're going, where we're all going—to the grave eventually. But I'm sure as hell not going to rush it! What matters is here and now, and right now I'm flirting with this big guy with a shaved head."

I was really impressed by the spiritual clarity embedded in her remark—her awareness that fearing and fretting and forward casting into all kinds of worries or situations kills the presence of now.

I can't remember whether it was George Burns or Paul Newman who said, "Nobody gets out of this life alive." So, like that lady in the nursing home reminds us, why don't we just get on with it, right now, as it is now? You know, the only folks who don't have any problems are those lying in your local graveyard. That's right—if you haven't got any problems or issues, you're dead.

Attentive curiosity is a mental position. It's a stance of being able to step back from whatever is going on and just look at it. As soon as you go into a curiosity state, fear can't follow because when you're observing something, your *thoughts* are in motion looking at whatever you're looking at but *you* are in stillness. You're not trying at that moment to solve your problems. No fear can exist when you become curious about why something is the way it is.

When you're attentively curious about the patterns of your life, you're not trying to control it. You're just looking at it. And when you see it clearly, then you can decide whether you want that circumstance in your life or not. It's like being in a clothing store and looking at a red sweater, taking in the color and how it fits with the rest of your wardrobe, and deciding,

"No, I don't think I'll buy it." So with attentive curiosity you can look at any circumstance in your life and decide, "No, I don't want that in my life anymore," or "Yes, I do want this in my life." You can't know what you want in your life if you don't know what you're looking at.

Attentive curiosity is the number one fallback position when you're in any kind of distress. You may find yourself saying "yes" when you really want to say "no." And then you get hard on yourself and start beating yourself up. But that isn't what this is about. Attentive curiosity is the faculty of your mind that shows you that there is always an alternate way of looking at things. And that leads to undulation in the context of your life as a whole.

Undulate into Another Way

Very often when we seek patterns of meaning in our lives, we want things to make sense immediately. We want all the pieces to fit. We want easy answers and fail-safe conclusions. However, life has a stubborn way of not fitting into easy answers and fail-safe conclusions. When you look at life through only one lens, I guarantee life will kick your butt into having to look at situations in a different way.

"What do you mean?" many people ask me. "Are you saying that we shouldn't have any core values?"

No, that is not what I mean. Yes, we have and need core values. They may differ from culture to culture and from person to person. For me a core value could be truthfulness. For you it could be compassion. For another person it might be justice. And indeed we all have more than one core value. If we follow a religious or spiritual tradition, our core values and our ethics will likely line up with that tradition. But even without a clearly defined spiritual tradition in your life, humankind is by nature spiritual in the sense that we are the only species that seeks meaning and purpose. Once you raise questions of meaning and purpose, once you start asking the big questions, you are in the realm of the spiritual.

A big part of the realm of the spiritual—and a part that is often missed by people who want to be dogmatic—is that there is much in life that is a mystery to us. Very often we just can't know the "why" of things. Neuroscientists today will be the first to tell you that there is much about the human brain that is not yet understood. Medical scientists will tell you that there are diseases the cause of which we don't yet understand. And every one of us, at one time or another in our lives, will ask the question, "Why is this happening?" whether about something happening to us or to others we know or hear about. What is the explanation for why innocent people get killed during wars? What is the explanation for why through no overt fault of your own you end up getting fired or your mate leaves you? Or as the title of a best-selling book by Rabbi Harold Kushner puts it, what is the explanation for "When Bad Things Happen to Good People"? Rabbi Kushner knows whereof he speaks. He had to face his own child's fatal illness.

Another variation on that theme is to turn it around and to ask also why *good* things happen. Good things can be equally mysterious. What is the explanation for why someone won a huge lottery? How did you happen to be in the right place and the right time to be picked for exactly the job you wanted? How did you happen to meet the love of your life in a bookstore you ran into to get out of the rain?

Sure, there are factual aspects we can point to. We can say that people get killed in wars because war involves using weapons and invading territories where there are innocent civilians. We can say that we got fired because our industry is going through a shakedown. We can say that hundreds of thousands of people died in a tsunami because they lived on coastal areas and tsunamis are an awesome force of nature. We can say that we won the lottery because we've been buying tickets regularly. We can say that we're more likely to find our soul mate in a bookstore because bookstores are important to us, too. We can say we got the job because our qualifications are right for it.

But none of that really answers the bigger why. The best we can do is point to certain circumstances. We can't really have any inkling into exactly why things happen the way they do. To me, that recognition is what spiritual undulation is all about. Sometimes we have to let our mind dance around all the possibilities. Sometimes our mind has to do the dance around the mystery itself. You don't know why something happened to you. But it did, and so now you undulate around it in order to discover how to integrate this experience into your life.

Sometimes you have to undulate around your own core values. This happens when you have an ethical dilemma that pits two or more of your core values against each other. For example, perhaps a core value for you is loyalty to friends and loved ones, and another core value is truthfulness. Let's say that you witnessed a friend of yours shoplifting. The store clerk becomes aware that something is missing, and she asks you, "Did you see who swiped that shirt?" Which core value do you call upon—the value to be truthful or the value to be loyal? Maybe your friend stole the article of clothing because he has been out of work and is really financially struggling. In that kind of situation, emotions are going to enter the picture.

What then? So you'll need to undulate for a time around those values, and part of the mystery of life is that no matter which answer you give in a case of conflicting values, you will not be wholly satisfied with it.

In other words, your relationship with any circumstance in your life can be viewed from more than one perspective in terms of assigning meaning and purpose to it. The energy of undulation reminds us not to get too attached to our own version of reality but to be continually aware that there are many possibilities and many truths we have not yet discovered in our own lives.

Clear Intent to Be as You Are

We all have so many different influences on our lives. Being who we are in any given moment can change with the circumstances of our lives. Take, for example, the person in training to be a soldier, the person in training to become a lawyer, the person becoming a really good athlete, the person in the process of becoming a good parent. After any amount of training, whether formally or from life experiences, you are a different person from what you were when you first started. The person you were before you started is still with you but that person has changed because of the added experiences.

So on the level of purpose and meaning and putting our lives together, we can't hang on to experiences or realities we experienced before. We can't focus our intent to be the way we were ten years ago, or last year, or even two hours ago. If your intent is to hold on to some elusive sense of permanence, it is an illusory intent. Clear intent, as I have come to apply it to spirituality in living my life, is the intent to be exactly who you are in this moment of time right now.

The warrior mind lives with the intent of being in the moment, neither ruminating on the past nor attempting to forecast the future. It is only in the now that you can scan your environment and notice what's going on around you. It's only in the now that you can experience your thoughts and your emotions. Brooding about the past and worrying about the future takes up a lot of energy and this drains the warrior mind. The warrior mind is always in the present and holds to a clear intent to be there. We only trip ourselves up when we hark back to the past or forward into the future.

Many people don't want to be in the present because they don't like the present they're in. They want to be thinner, they want to be richer, they want not to have to go through that divorce, they want not to have to get up every day at 6 A.M., and so forth. So many of us spend a lot of time thinking about all the things in our present that we don't like, and we escape from that by going back into the past or projecting ourselves into the future. "If only I had done things differently" and "If I can achieve such and such a goal in the future, everything will be okay" are two of the most depleting mind-sets you could ever have.

I'm not saying that we should never think about the past, for indeed the past teaches us many lessons. And I'm not saying we should never make plans for the future. But there's a big difference between the warrior mind and the undisciplined mind. The warrior mind knows that all thought occurs in the present, including thoughts of the past or the future. The warrior mind directs thought from the platform of the present. So many times when we think of the future—for example, of some goal we want to achieve or some change we want to make—we find our mind gets lost in that scenario until we lose touch with the present. That's not the warrior mind. The warrior mind knows that the seeds of the future are in the present and that the past remains with us in our memories, but that all we have at any point in time is right now. "Upon those who step into the same rivers, different and again different waters flow," wrote the ancient historian Heraclitus.

Make it your clear intent always to be in the now of your own life.

Grappling with the Gods

Someone once asked the great Jungian analyst James Hillman what the purpose of life was. "To serve the gods," he answered. By "gods" Hillman meant the energies, archetypes, and intuitions in our lives that call us toward what our unique purpose is, to the unfolding of our own unique personhood and our own talents and strengths.

Many people today do not have a sense of even where their talents or strengths lie. We allow other people to determine our life's purpose for us—the son who decides to be a doctor because his parents always wanted a doctor in the family; the woman who works at a job she really doesn't like all that much because she doesn't believe there could ever be a job in the field she is really interested in; the man who becomes a stockbroker but really wants to be an artist and in being a stockbroker eventually forgets about the artist inside him.

So often we abandon our dreams. So often we give up the most vital parts of ourselves in the name of practicality. And then we wonder why we are living in such a culture of discontent. But, as Hillman points out in his writings, particularly in *The Soul's Code*, the "gods" are not easily placated. They are not easily denied. And so into our lives creeps a sense of dissatisfaction, the inner voice that says, "You know, I'm not really happy with what I'm doing." And the minute you acknowledge that feeling, you are grappling with the gods.

You can choose to run away from that grappling. You can slip back into resignation and denial, or you can choose to really take on the question, to really grapple with what it is you want in your life. You can choose to take on the quest for your life's purpose.

What stops us from grappling with our lives? What stops us from engaging in finding out who we are and what we want? Very often, it's fear. When I begin teaching people in the martial arts, they say something like, "I want to learn to carry less fear in my life."

Acknowledging fear and then learning to lay it down is part of the process of being completely human, completely whole in ourselves. Each time we master a fear, we have grown. Most fears, when we really put them to the test, are found to not really exist other than in our imaginations or in our perceptions of what we think the outside reality is. Very often, fear is merely False Evidence Appearing Real.

One of my fears has always been snakes. I've always had a very healthy respect for these critters—I just didn't want to get too close to them. When Leah, a friend of mine who is an expert on dolphins, had my wife and me over to her home, what should I discover but that she had a pet python named Cirrus. Leah uses the snake in teaching classes to people about animal awareness and gaining familiarity with species we might not otherwise encounter. She said to me, "If you like, I'll put Cirrus over your shoulders."

My first thought was, "Whoa! This is a python we're talking about!" A whole lot of other thoughts ran through my head, not the least of which was a consideration of what I would do if this eight-foot snake decided to choke me or crush my head. But here I was, this martial artist and former soldier, and I didn't want to betray my fears. So I said, "Sure, go ahead." I have to tell you that there is an unusually eerie feeling about a snake slowly wrapping itself around your shoulders and head. I remember the smooth feel of the snakeskin and I could feel the vibrating of his body. I had every faith that Leah knew her pet snake well enough and also that Cirrus had had a lot of experience being around humans.

That afternoon I lost a lot of my fear of snakes. That doesn't mean that I plan to go sauntering up to rattlesnakes or boa constrictors to establish close personal contact with them the way I did with Cirrus. But I realized that sometimes what scares us is simply the unfamiliar and that sometimes it's good to make the acquaintance of the unfamiliar.

Let's say you've been repressing a lot of your dreams and hopes; you've set your wishes aside in favor of a life path that has not energized you. In all likelihood, at the point where you first feel the urgings of your discontent and begin to grapple with them, some of the stuff that comes to your consciousness may seem scary and unfamiliar, just as Cirrus was scary and unfamiliar to me. It may seem damn scary to really consider that you could be an artist and not an accountant. Or that you could climb Mount Kilimanjaro. Or that you could play the piano. Or that you could woo the sweetheart of your dreams and he or she would really say yes to you.

That's the profound lesson that Cirrus taught me: that the unfamiliar can be scary but it can also be exhilarating to reach out and embrace that uncertainty, to take hold of it and really look at it. I'm glad I said yes to the Cirrus experience.

Let's assume that you want to discover what your life's purpose is, that you want to grapple with the gods. If you're looking outward, you're looking in the wrong place. When you are presented in your life with a major and significant challenge, rest assured that everything previously in your life—every adventure you have ever had, every trauma you have ever experienced, every happy event you have ever enjoyed, every dream you have ever dreamed—has given you the ability to cultivate the energy to handle the stress, challenge, or issue *from inside yourself* the moment it lands on your plate.

Rolling Waves and Surfing the Tides of Life

There are two things about ocean tides. The first is that they continually change from high tide to low tide and back again and the tidal floor never looks the same one day as it did the day before. The second is that the tides are eternal. Every ocean upon the earth participates in the ageless process of tidal motion, in and out.

When you surf the tides of your life, those tides change. Tides go out and tides come in. There are times in our lives when we will be at low tide. Other times we will be at high tide. And there is all the space in between. The image of the rolling waves is a wonderful analogy to put us in touch with the knowledge that life is a process of continual flow.

Often when we've got a nagging sensation of being stuck or of being frustrated, we are damming up our own flow. There is so much in society today to interrupt our flow—loud city noises, demanding jobs with long hours, difficult relationships, continual bombardment by media and the electronic universe. It's not surprising that many people today are taking up yoga and meditational practices in order to help restore the inner quietness that will make them hear their own inner flow.

I recall seeing a mural on a restaurant wall in Santa Monica, California, that said, "You can find absolute truth in silence. Failing that, try music." In silence, you find things of great beauty. In silence, you get in touch with the flow of your life, with the rolling waves that carry energy to you and then carry your spent-up energy back out, only to return it to you again.

Many of the most meaningful, magical experiences of our lives come to us in silence. There's not a lot of talking going on when you're in the middle of a passionate kiss. When you're watching stars in the sky on a clear summer night out in the countryside, you're silenced into wonderment. When you're on a ship and the moon comes up on the horizon of the ocean, in your soul you touch the meeting of that celestial body with this celestial body, which is the Earth. The sheer beauty of it stuns you into silence.

And, as the Santa Monica restaurant mural says, if that doesn't work for you, try music.

The analogy of rolling waves helps you keep your mind open both to new possibilities and to gaining new insights into experiences you've already had and into the patterns that occur in your life. If you have an open mind to the energy of flow, you're not going to miss anything. You're going to be able to fully enjoy all the idiosyncrasies. You'll come off the top of a roller coaster and really feel that huge downward rush of speed and air—for truth be told, some of the rolling waves in our lives do feel more like a roller coaster than an ocean— but it's all waves.

And, Finally, the Whirlwind

In the big picture of your life, the whirlwind is transformation. It's the energy you feel when your life takes a sudden U-turn or you take a fork in the road you never thought you would ever travel. But don't confuse the whirlwind with being blind-sided. Remember that, as we have discussed, the whirlwind is a targeted energy. It's a pull-out-all-the stops energy. It's when *you* decide to make that U-turn in your life or go down that untraveled road.

It's when you give everything you've got to following your dreams. It's when you give everything you've got to battling an illness. It's when you give everything you've got to meeting your challenges.

In a very real sense, the entire way of the Shadow Warrior is a whirlwind path. Why? Because the path of the Shadow Warrior is a path of transformation and transformation is a whirlwind energy. All of the other five energy moves combine to make the whirlwind. And the warrior walks in that energy, only he walks in the calm "eye of the storm," where all is still and silent. It doesn't look like a whirlwind or feel like a whirlwind when you're in that calm eye center, but if you're walking your life there, you are transforming everything about yourself and your world. You have become the whirlwind.

In the way of the Shadow Warrior, you walk with the knowledge that all the knowledge of the universe is available to you. You just don't get it all at one time. The universe won't give Shadow Warriors more information than they can handle at the time. When you live in the calm mind of the warrior—awake, aware, and attentive—you understand those periods when staying silent is appropriate. You understand when to speak. You understand when to defend. You understand when to walk away. You understand not to do violence to yourself by criticizing yourself and beating yourself up for your perceived mistakes.

You learn to resolve conflict by winning your battles as much as possible without hurting others. The warrior of merit wins battles without anyone else feeling defeat and before others even realized that a battle is taking place. That's right—if you practice the six energy moves—attentive curiosity, undulation, clear intent, grappling, rolling waves, and the whirlwind—and bring these images and disciplines into your life, you will find that you'll be able to anticipate a battle or conflict and be able to take action to prevent it from happening. You will have made the transition from warrior to peacemaker and peacekeeper in your life. You will step out of the shadow of fear.

Standing in this center of who you are and surrounded by the energies of the six moves, you stand in the energy flow of your present moment. And where do you go from here? As I wrote on a card to my wife on her most recent birthday, "Happy birthday, and ever forward, my love, to the here and now."

Reminders to Your Warrior Mind

1. It is human nature to ask questions of meaning and purpose, particularly at those times in our lives when we feel under siege. When we feel we're beyond our own capacities and beyond our limits, we look for a source larger than ourselves to give us the energy and the strength to get through the challenging situation.

2. Our innate instinct to seek meaning is what we call "spiritual." But "spiritual" does not just mean specific religions or belief systems. It's a far wider concept—it's the energy that causes us to seek for patterns in our lives and to plug our own energy system into an energy flow that is all around us.

3. The warrior mind is ultimately about seeking peace. There is an expression in the martial arts world that says, "The warrior of merit wins the battle without causing others to feel defeat." Though there are times when we will be required to "fight to win," the warrior mind sees overt conflict as the last resort and that you do everything possible to redirect negative energies. Your aim is not to defeat your enemy. It is to use the energies in the situation to restore harmony to both yourself and the environment.

4. From a spiritual perspective, think of attentive curiosity as "beginner's mind." An interesting exercise is to experiment with looking at everything as if you have never seen it before, as if you are a "Martian" who has to go back to Mars and explain what you saw on Earth. It is amazing the wonderments you will see when you look at the familiar through the eyes of imagining you are seeing it for the first time.

5. Life contains many mysteries and puzzles. Things happen that we cannot explain. Learning to undulate around the questions and to dance around possibilities can alter your relationship with the circumstances of your life. Make it your clear intent always to be in the now of your own life.

6. Too often we allow other people to determine or influence our life's purpose. However, the only way you will find your own unique purpose is to grapple with it yourself. Not only can "grappling with the gods" help us find a sense of meaning, but also the energy of rolling waves will help us surf the time and tides of our own lives. The image of rolling waves is a wonderful analogy to put us in touch with the knowledge that life is a process of continual flow. And last, as we see our life as a series of transformations, we realize that the path of the Shadow Warrior is the whirlwind itself. The warrior of merit walks in that energy, only in the calm eye of the storm. If you're living from that place of peace with all the energies swirling around you, yet your center remaining grounded and clear, you're transforming yourself and your world.

Resources for the Warrior Mind

Mindfulness

The practice of mindfulness, of being fully aware in the present and calming the mind, is a foundational aspect of the six energies. There are many meditation centers across North America that teach mindfulness meditation. Many have informative websites you can find by typing "mindfulness meditation" into your search engine. As well, there are many books, CDs, and videos on the topic. Check your local bookstore.

Here are a couple of suggestions as a starting point:

- The work of Jon Kabat-Zinn is well respected. Kabat-Zinn teaches mindfulness meditative practices in the context of health and well-being. He is the author of several books. You can find more information about Kabat-Zinn, his books, practice, and meditational tapes and CDs on the website of the Center for Mindfulness in Medicine, Health Care, and Society (CFM). The CFM website is www.umassmed.edu/cfm.

- Jack Kornfield is one of the most prominent teachers of Vipassana (mindfulness) in the Western

Hemisphere. He is associated with the Spirit Rock Meditation Center. Spirit Rock has many well-known meditation teachers and lots of good information on its website (www.spiritrock.org).

Self-Defense

The chapter on physical self-defense may lead some readers to want to know more. Many communities offer self-defense classes in schools, community agencies, or martial arts studios. One particularly good website with lots of great information on the topic is www.nononsenseselfdefense.com.

Martial Arts

If you are interested in pursuing a specific martial art, check out www.martialinfo.com. This website is chock full of information about the martial arts, complete with a state-by-state and province-by-province listing of martial arts training centers and teachers.

Index

About the Author

Jim Pritchard is a successful businessman and security adviser, and a speaker and teacher of both psychological and physical self-defense and conflict resolution. He is a veteran of Special Forces and holds black belts in several martial arts, including the advanced practices of Ninjitsu and Taijitsu. His martial arts path involves the ways of the Shadow Warrior—advanced levels of self-awareness, stealth, and spiritual training.

Jim has taught physical and psychological defense to diverse groups of people, including high school teachers wanting to learn more effective communication techniques, and survivors of sexual assault (through the YWCA). He has conducted safety training and demonstrations to professional groups such as the Ontario Road Authority, and he has been involved as a consultant in human resources and training for industrial manufacturing and distribution companies in both Canada and the United States. As the founder and owner of his own business, Kit-Fast Solutions Inc., Jim was recently named an honored professional in the nationwide register of Who's Who (executive and business category).

For many years, Jim taught students of martial arts and self-defense at Hatashita Martial Arts Center in Kitchener, Ontario, in collaboration with Wayne Erdman, a former Olympic athlete and Pan-Am gold medalist, with whom Jim has trained and practiced for over two decades. "Jim extends the energy practices outside the realm of martial arts so that anyone can easily learn these and use them in their lives," says Erdman. "I think this is a very effective way of helping people build confidence and strength inside themselves to cope with almost any situation."

Since retiring from the business world in 2004, Jim spends most of his time conducting workshops, teaching life skills to individuals, and speaking to groups about fear and conflict resolution. He can be reached at life_skills@sympatico.ca or through his website, www.thewarriormind.com.